Pilgrims on a Journey

AKRON MENNONITE CHURCH
1959-2009

A SOCIAL HISTORY

GERALD W. KAUFMAN

PILGRIMS ON A JOURNEY
AKRON MENNONITE CHURCH
1959-2009

A Social History by
Gerald W. Kaufman

Library of Congress Number: 2009905149

International Standard Book Number: 978-1-60126-185-4

Printed 2009 at
Masthof Press
219 Mill Road
Morgantown, PA 19543-9516

Dedication

    This book is dedicated to the 46 courageous charter members of Akron Mennonite Church who got us started on our journey 50 years ago. Their foresight, inspiration, and wisdom have been an important source of guidance to us. You are now passing the torch to a new generation of pilgrims. Special mention is made of **Clarence Brubaker, Edna Byler, J.N. Byler, Savilla Diener, Ura Gingerich, Kathy Hostetler, Melvin Lapp, Loretta Leatherman, Louise Leatherman, Albert Miller, Esther Miller,** and **Robert Miller,** charter members who have now completed their earthly journey.

PILGRIMS ON A JOURNEY DVD

A video entitled **Pilgrims on a Journey** is included with this book. Charter members tell the story of Akron Mennonite Church in the transition from Monterey to the Brownstown Fire Hall. Persons who have served as congregational chairs of Akron Mennonite Church reflect on changes in theology, worship and mission during the 50-year history of AMC, and pastors comment on their years of service.

The video includes five chapters: Beginning, Church in the Early Days, Charter Member Stories, Congregational Chairs, and Pastors. To play individual chapters click "menu" on TV remote and select chapters.

Produced by Bob Wyble

Contents

Foreword

We all know that the main purpose for going to church is to worship God. It is important for the person leading worship to help us focus our attention on God when we sing *O Master, let me walk with thee, . . .*

We consider October 4, 1959, as the beginning of Akron Mennonite Church (AMC). On April 3 the first membership commitment was drawn up. I have had the privilege of worshiping in many churches —in Russia, in Canada, in England with Quakers, in Holland, Germany, Switzerland, South America, and other countries. Without hesitation I can say that when my wife Elfrieda and I were in the Akron Mennonite Church, we felt as close to God as in any other church. We had the privilege of being there for 28 years, the longest we lived anywhere in our almost 60 years of marriage.

AMC is well organized with many committees to carry out the work of the church. The belief in Jesus Christ is central, and *Nachfolge*, following Jesus Christ in daily life, is an essential part of membership. That is why only adults are baptized and received on a voluntary basis as church members. The author says: "Today we list 466 members, ten times more than we had at the beginning."

One of the central faith statements is the belief in peace and justice. Later you will come across the statement that *we can hardly get through a Sunday service without hearing 'peace and justice' mentioned.* I stood before Judge Burges in Manchester, England, held out both my arms, and said, "Your honor, you want to handcuff me and send me to prison or ship me back to Canada? You may do so. I will not become a soldier and kill another person." Peace is important to this body of believers.

Because of the Mennonite Central Committee (MCC) headquarters being also located in Akron, Pennsylvania, and this organization having a constant flow of volunteers, it was to be expected that our AMC membership would likewise fluctuate to some degree. Some were with MCC for three or more years and then left to serve abroad or somewhere else. While they were with MCC in Akron, many attended AMC.

This part of Pennsylvania is known for the location of the Amish. Whether that had anything to do with our desire for a simple life, I do not know. In my background in Russia and Canada (1914-1941), the simple life was not emphasized. But in this book the author says of the people at AMC: *We were pilgrims who wanted to live simply, to remain small in size, to be faithful to the large Mennonite church, and to choose carefully our dose of piety.*

To live simply and to remain small has not always been easy. Since the beginning in 1959 there have been 911 persons join AMC. Some have created new church groups with locations at the MCC Welcoming Center and in the city of Lancaster. In order to have members relate to each other, as Paul advises in a *mutually affectionate* way, small groups have been established, a coffee break is a regular feature for Sunday morning, and people continue to meet in small groups in their homes. Gerald Kaufman highlights the strengths of AMC—its blend of so many different members from all over North America and its mixture of different personalities, languages, theological orientations and life styles.

It is obvious that if we are looking for one word to describe the future of AMC, it is the word *change*. However, in spite of outward changes that will inevitably come if AMC remains Christ-centered, following the teachings and example of Jesus it will remain a unique and vital church.

- Peter Dyck

Preface

This is the story of a 50-year-old church, Akron Mennonite Church. When compared with many other congregations, we are young. Even though our *congregation* is young, many of our *charter members* are now in their senior years. Some have made the *Ultimate Journey.* One of them, Kathy Hostetler, who played a very important role throughout our history, died somewhat unexpectedly on March 28, 2009. She and her husband John served on one of the *decade teams* doing important archival work for this book. Indeed, she was the first person I would contact when I needed more information. My last call to her was just about ten days before her death.

I have not written this story as a precise chronology. It will not read like a diary might. Even 50 years is too long a time to retell a history in detail. In every one of the 2,600 weeks as a congregation, something happened that could have been included in this book. More than 900 people have had an important connection with this church over the years. That's enough stories and plenty of people to fill several volumes.

Originally I had planned to present just the broader story of the church and to name only some of the most significant participants. I wanted to avoid the tedium that can come from including too many names in the narrative. I also wanted to reduce the chances of offending people whose names might have been left out inadvertently. Bowing to the suggestions of one of my advisors, I agreed to include more names and details. It was his belief that details can provide more color for readers and more data for serious historians. Originally I had planned to only tell the *what* in our story. He thought that it would be important to tell the *why* as well. I think he was right.

I give credit to hymn 307 in our *Worship Book* for the "Pilgrims on a Journey" theme. It came to me one morning as I awakened. I couldn't get the song out of my mind until I chose those words from the second verse for the book title. I think the Pilgrim motif fits our people. Always a bit on the edge of the American mainstream, we at AMC—*sans* black Pilgrim's clothes and Plymouth Rock—behave very much like Pilgrims. With a touch of piety, simplicity, and a deep commitment to following Christ, we fit the part very well. Being the world citizens that we are, our members have been—and will continue to be—on a journey. Perhaps fearing that we will get too comfortable in middle class North America, some of us live with our suitcases packed ready for a new journey. It is my hope that what follows in the book will capture, at least, some of that spirit.

Now, a word about some of the pilgrims who joined me on my book-writing journey. First, my wife Marlene served as the unofficial *coordinator* and *motivator* for the project. She is much more organized than I am and compiled stacks of data and stories to allow me to concentrate on the writing. Without her in that role, I might still be writing at the time of our centennial!

My editor Naomi Wyble was not only grammarian-in-chief, but as good editors can do, gently nudged me to have the manuscript make sense. When I became too subjective in my writing, she helped me to take a step back to see the broader picture. As the project progressed her quiet enthusiasm was encouraging. When the final manuscript was completed, proofreader Anita Brendle gave it a final review to make sure the rest of us weren't missing some obvious mistakes.

Our church administrator Janet Weber was unfailingly patient when we made our many calls for more information from the archives and her computer. She was always willing to take time out of her busy schedule to provide the facts that we were seeking. She was also very helpful in opening up the archives to our panel of *decade teams* who did the primary review of the bulletins, annual reports, and other important data. The information they gathered was priceless, and their summaries will now be placed in the archives for future use. Those researchers were; John and Kathy Hostetler, Sam Wenger, Sam and Dorcas Rolon, Anita Brendle, Don Mellinger, and H.A. Penner. Flo Harnish served as a roving researcher. Priscilla Ziegler, Church Historian, was important in bringing the time-line up to date.

I am also grateful to Naomi Wyble for selecting, organizing, and deciding on the placement of the pictures in this book. The synergy between the text and the pictures is remarkable. The pictures put a human face on some very important stories. H.A. Penner was especially helpful in supplying more recent pictures. Memory Album coordinator Bonnie Stauffer and her predecessors made the process so much easier by organizing pictures in the albums. And I am also indebted to numerous persons who have given me stories to use, and who were available to receive my persistent calls for *just a bit more information.*

The Anniversary Committee members—Bob Wyble (Chair), Renny Magill, Ed Miller, and Janet Weber—were supportive throughout the process. Special mention is made of the creative work of Bob Wyble for the production of the DVD that is found on the inside of the back cover of the book. This may be the first time that a written text was accompanied by a DVD for a church history! The first-person stories he gathered could not have been told adequately in print.

Dennis Stoesz, Archivist at the Mennonite Church USA Archives, Goshen, Indiana, was very welcoming to his sanctuary on the Goshen College campus. He provided boxfuls of material about various items we were researching, including a fascinating account of our first—and only—Bishop, O.N. Johns. A special moment occurred on our trip to Goshen when, while staying in the home of my brother Melvin and his wife Lois, they invited their good friend David Johns—son of O.N. Johns—to join us for dinner. He was able to fill in some pieces of his father's life that we never would have known otherwise.

At the tail end of this project, I was honored to have John and Kathy Hostetler, Sam Wenger and Lester Graybill critique my manuscript. Brinton Rutherford, historian from the Lancaster Mennonite Conference, was also extraordinarily helpful in his review. These persons made some important corrections that, I hope, authenticate the work.

Finally, I thank Lois Ann Mast of Masthof Press for her skillfulness in bringing all of this effort to print. The design and the logo are evidence of her creativity.

I ask for your forgiveness if I have overlooked important stories and names. I have made a sincere effort to get the details as accurate as possible. The information in the book was gathered through the end of 2008. Generally, more recent data was not included. It is my hope that this book will be helpful in understanding the Pilgrim people who have created and sustained AMC. I invite you to celebrate with us at this important milestone on our journey.

- Gerald W. Kaufman

Chapter One

The Pilgrimage to Akron

T here we were on October 4, 1959—89 adults and children gathered in the Fire Hall in Brownstown, Pennsylvania—for our first worship service. As a newly emerging congregation we were beginning a journey. Most of us were leaving behind our mother church, Monterey Mennonite, some ten miles down the road, to become a

October 4, 1959, Photo 1—Row 1: Paul Leatherman, Loretta Leatherman, Alverta Martin, Ginny Lapp, Louise Leatherman, Warren Leatherman, Ura Gingerich, Gladys Gingerich, Clarence Brubaker. Row 2: Dwight Wiebe with Christine, Margot Wiebe, Lydia Weber, Mel Lapp, Lester Weber with Steve, Edgar Stoesz, 3 unidentified, J.N. Byler, 1 unidentified.

church of our own. In many ways we were as hymn 307 in our *Worship Book* proclaims, *pilgrims on a journey.* This was our first day on that journey.

But were we pilgrims? We were certainly not like the Pilgrims who settled in Massachusetts in 1620. That caricature hardly fit us. And we weren't a people who made pilgrimages to holy sites, as some Muslims and Catholics do. But if the dictionary definition of a pilgrim is *to wander*, that was accurate. From our beginning we have, indeed, been wanderers.

Not that we were the first people, however, to wander. Many years ago Abraham, in an act of faith, journeyed to the Land of Canaan. Indeed, the Children of Abraham have constantly been on the move. In the Diaspora, Jewish people scattered throughout the world, as have Abraham's Islamic descendents.

October 4, 1959, Photo 2—Row 1: Grace Brubaker with Sue, Edna Byler, Erma Swartzentruber, 1 unidentified, Savilla Diener, Menno Diener, David Hess with John, Ruth Hess. Row 2: Vera Smoker, Earl Bowman with David, Rosemary Shenk, Jim Millen, 1 unidentified, Joy Millen, Emma Keens, 2 unidentified, Kathy Hostetler, John Hostetler, Hannele Suter, Beulah Raber and Merrill Raber.

The early Christian church missionaries were also on the move when they spread the Gospel throughout the Middle East, Europe, and beyond. In our own history as Anabaptists, our ancestors journeyed to America to escape persecution, to avoid being assimilated into the European culture, and for economic reasons. The Apostle Paul in Hebrews 13:14 reminds us, "Here on Earth we have no continuing place but we seek one to come." Indeed, no *place* is ever permanent.

About half of the people gathered in Brownstown on this date weren't native to Lancaster County. We had come from other parts of the United States and Canada and some to work at Mennonite Central Committee, an Anabaptist relief agency based in Akron, Pennsylvania. Several of us had come here to work at a shoe factory—Miller, Hess and Company, Inc. One of its owners, Orie Miller, originally from Indiana, was also a founder of MCC. Still others from our group chose to come here to pursue careers in this community.

Before arriving in Akron several of us had lived overseas as missionaries, while others had served in the Pax program as an alternative to being drafted into military service. Several of us had served stateside in Civilian Public Service camps. One person volunteered to be a herdsman on a cattle boat delivering dairy cows to war-stricken countries in Europe.

But others of us here in Brownstown weren't on a journey that could be measured by miles traveled. We were born and raised in Lancaster County. Our journey was a spiritual one. We were leaving behind some of the conservativeness of our Lancaster Mennonite Conference congregations. Our journey led us to a congregation that allowed more freedom in the ways we practiced our faith.

For most of us, Brownstown was actually a second stop on this journey. The first stop had been at Monterey Mennonite, a church that was only thirteen years old by the time we left to form our group in Brownstown. Monterey had been a safe haven for us. It was the most compatible alternative available for us. We didn't fit in well with the Lancaster Conference churches because of lifestyle differences, including the ways we dressed, and the fact that some of us wore jewelry. Indeed, these differences kept us from being served communion in their churches. Church historian and theologian John Ruth says the local churches found the people at Monterey to be "startling, if not downright offensive."

Their resistance, however, is easy to understand. We were establishing a new Mennonite presence in the middle of a church community that had been here from the early 1700s. They and the Franconia Mennonite Conference, forty miles to the east, had been *the* Mennonite church in America many years before other communities like the ones we had come from were settled. We were interlopers in a rather homogenous community at a critical time in its history.

The local Mennonite churches were already losing members to emerging independent congregations. Their members were being influenced, in part, by the new medium of Christian radio. Restlessness was spreading throughout the Lancaster Conference. It is understandable why the presence of an entirely new Mennonite alternative in their midst was troubling.

Monterey Mennonite Church, 1959.

Ura and Gladys Gingerich's basement, Paul Ruth, Marge Ruth, Virginia Lapp, and Melvin Lapp, October 1961.

Starting our own church in Brownstown was not our only choice, however. Several years earlier, a General Conference Mennonite congregation had begun meeting at the YMCA in Lancaster city. Eventually that group would establish a congregation (Bethel Mennonite) on the west side of the city of Lancaster. They were similar to our group in lifestyle and we could have found acceptance there. However, none of us leaving Monterey affiliated with Bethel, mostly because it was located too far away from where we lived. In addition, the General Conference practices were too progressive at that time for some of us.

Nevertheless, the impulse to establish a new church was stirring within us. Not surprisingly, our parting from Monterey was painful, especially for our friends who chose to stay behind. At first they weren't convinced that starting a new church was necessary. However, after much discussion—and some healing—the members at Monterey blessed our church-planting efforts as symbolized by their gift of $3,339 for our building fund.

The decision to form a new congregation was unanimous among the group who gathered those first months. Enthusiasm was high in our planning meetings. The basement of Ura and Gladys Gingerich became our venue for decision-making. One of the first decisions was to purchase land in Akron where we would build our church. One of our hopes, however, was that we would be a positive witness in our new community. We wanted to be evangelical and even considered eliminating the word *Mennonite* from our congregational name. Eventually the decision was made to keep our identity within the Mennonite denomination and we assumed the name *Akron Mennonite Church*.

We would call the Brownstown Fire Hall our home for a period of three-and-one-half years. We rented space there until we could build our church. There is a small touch of irony that we, the spiritual descendents of martyrs who were burned at the stake in Switzerland, were meeting in a fire hall. The siren sounded a few times during our services but we continued worshiping undaunted. The fires of the martyrs had long ago been lost from our memories. We felt fortunate just to have a place to meet.

Leola Fire Hall; leaving after service: Ginny, Seth, and Charles Ebersole; J.N. Byler; and Rollin, Betty, and Rich Rheinheimer, 1959.

Obviously the surroundings weren't elegant. No stained glass windows. No organ. Not even benches like we had at Monterey. But the décor didn't bother us because as Mennonites we don't expect to worship in cathedrals. Our ancestors in Switzerland and Germany chose to worship in caves, barns, and private homes. Here in the States most of us were accustomed to worshiping in simple buildings that are sometimes referred to as meetinghouses.

Thus, on October 4, 1959, we held our first worship service. Pastor Glenn Esh from Monterey served as our part-time pastor until

Ura Gingerich and Glenn Weaver, 1962.

Choir at Brownstown with Warren Leatherman as leader, January 1962.

we secured Kermit Derstine as our pastor in August 1961. We needed to start our worship service at 9:00 a.m. to allow Pastor Esh to return to Monterey for their 10:30 a.m. service. It is interesting that 50 years later our starting time remains at 9:00 a.m. Several attempts were made through the years to change the time for worship but 9:00 a.m. remains imprinted on our psyche. Traditions can rather quickly become hidebound.

Despite the fact that we borrowed Glenn Esh from Monterey to be our pastor, we had the full responsibility to run our new church. That meant leading our singing, lifting our offerings, teaching our Sunday School classes, and doing all the other things churches do. Few of us had exercised this kind of leadership in a church before. We were, for the most part, in our 30s and 40s and had young families. In fact, there were only three senior citizens and one baptized teenager among our initial membership.

As with all new groups we learned to adjust as we went along. People quickly assumed roles. Edna and J.N. Byler became the unof-

Sunday School class, from left to right: Jill Miller, Esther Miller, Duane Gingerich, Grace Diener, and James Hess, 1959.

ficial parents of our fledgling church. Among other things Edna made sure the monthly fellowship meals were served on time. That meant asking teacher Esther Miller and her small flock of youth to vacate their classroom in the kitchen. We appointed a treasurer, selected officers, and formed a building committee. We were governed by a group of five men, called the advisory committee. We incorporated, chose an official name, and erected a church building—heady things for young and free-spirited pilgrims to do.

Everyone was involved in setting the direction for the church. No members sat on the sidelines. We drew up our first membership commitment April 3, 1960. It was a rather demanding document that, among other things, expected members to be present at all meetings, including worship and Sunday School. We promised each other to be open to giving and receiving counsel. Several years later we were also expected to join one of the new House Church groups that were being formed. This kind of submission to the will of each other seems rather remarkable in the individualistic world that we are now a part of.

Even though we took our membership commitment seriously, our group wasn't overly restrictive otherwise. Here nobody measured

Jae (J.N.) and Edna Ruth Byler, 1959.

Brownstown Fire Hall: Seth Ebersole, Esther Horst, and Gladys and Edgar Stoesz, 1961.

At Brownstown: Loretta Leatherman, Joy Millen, Marjorie Ruth, Irma Bowman, and Gladys Gingerich, 1961.

skirts and none of the men, except Pastor Glenn Esh, wore plain suits. Most women wore the devotional head covering as was common in the broader *Old* Mennonite church at that time. Within our worship service, we resisted the use of musical instruments to accompany our singing.

However, reflecting the *in the world, but not of the world* struggle that was a part of being Mennonite at that time, we studied the place of modern intrusions in the home, such as radio and television. We expressed a real concern about other new developments in the larger culture. We might have moved past the Lancaster Conference in some of our practices, but not as far as we might have thought. Remaining separate from *the world* was on our minds too.

What was most important was that we had given birth to a church! We could take communion! We were among people who were more like us. Our Bishop, O.N. Johns from Louisville, Ohio, was a kind, diplomatic man who was instrumental in connecting Monterey,

Neffsville, and now Brownstown/Akron with the Ohio and Eastern Mennonite Conference. That affiliation would give us an official connection with the broader Mennonite church from which many of us had come. This conference membership remained until 1978 when the Atlantic Coast Mennonite Conference was established for the eastern Mennonite churches. This regional conference took the place of the Ohio and Eastern Mennonite Conference.

Considering the distance that Bishop Johns had traveled to provide oversight, it is rather remarkable that he could play such an important

Ura Gingerich, Paul Leatherman, and O.N. Johns, 1959.

role in helping us to get started. What made it even more significant is that at one point he served 28 congregations in Ohio, Pennsylvania, New York and Maryland. At the peak of his bishopric oversight he spent more than 300 days in one year away from his home. In 1967, John I. Smucker, who was then referred to as Overseer, replaced him and the title *Bishop* disappeared from use at AMC.

The small group gathered at Brownstown began a journey of our own choosing. We were pilgrims who wanted to live simply, to remain small in size, to be faithful to the larger Mennonite Church, and to choose carefully our dose of piety. We knew where we had come from. We had high hopes for where we were going. We had indeed purchased land in Akron, upon which we would build our new church.

We were affected by the optimism that was sweeping the broader American culture in the early days of the 1960s. The *New Frontier*, the space race, and the idealism brought by President Kennedy pulsed through our veins. We were looking ahead with only a scant look backward. Our destination might not always have been clear, but we had little doubt about the direction of our journey. We were young, idealistic, and maybe a bit naïve. We had come this far and wouldn't be deterred from being God's presence in our new community. We had formed a church that was unique and sufficient to meet our needs. Although our journey had at times been somewhat unsteady, we were pointed forward. That journey continues 50 years later.

Chapter Two

Pilgrims: Numbers and Characteristics

In our first gathering 50 years ago, it was clear that we were a young group. Most of us were in the early stages of raising families. Of the 89 adults and children who gathered for the first worship service, forty-six—including Ed Miller who was then in his teens—would sign up as charter members on May 8, 1960. Within a year of that initial sign-in, ten more people joined. Two of them were spouses of charter members who had to miss the original registration to stay home with sick children.

Today we list 466 members, more than ten times greater than we had in the beginning. Our growth has been steady, averaging about seventeen new members per year. The year in which the most growth took place was 1979 when 39 members were added. Of that number, 27 were youth. The largest collective surge in growth was in the years from 1979 through 1981 when 90 persons joined AMC. The next largest growth was between the years of 1965 through 1967 when 83 persons joined. Our lowest years for growth were 1968 (3), 1996 (6), and 2008 (5). New members have been added either through transferring from another congregation or by being baptized at AMC.

MYF trip to Hawk Mountain, left to right: Phil Leatherman, Daryl Hurst, Jim Millen, David Hess, and Ed Miller, 1961.

These membership numbers reflect *net growth;* that is, our total number of members after subtracting members who died or who transferred to other churches. Over AMC's 50-year history, 47 members died and 200 members transferred to other churches. The *net growth* line has been consistently upward. By most membership standards, we are now a large congregation.

However, it has become increasingly difficult to know what the *membership* numbers mean when they are compared to the *attendance* numbers. What complicates the meaning of these numbers is that in our Anabaptist tradition, only baptized youth and adults are eligible to be members. *Attendance* numbers include the members and all others who are present for the worship service.

In the early years attendance exceeded membership. In 1962 there were 62 members and 162 attenders. By 1968 the membership and attender numbers were approximately the same. Today the ratio is much different. Even though we now have 466 members, on average about 270 people attend worship. As expected, attendance is higher when there are special events and lower at other times, particularly in the summer.

What is clear is that we have many more members than we have people in attendance. Although the membership number has climbed steadily over the 50 years, the rate of increase has slowed in recent years. Attendance on the other hand, peaked at an average of 350 per Sunday, about ten years ago. Since then it has been on a steady decline.

Over the years, AMC has served an indeterminate number of people who called it their church home, if even for a brief time. Some have moved to the Akron community to work at MCC while others have come to Lancaster County in connection with their careers. A smaller number of attenders have been from the local community and visit for a period of time to determine whether AMC is a right fit for them. Some of these people attend regularly and some occasionally. The church is a spiritual point of reference for a variety of attenders, albeit a marginal one for some of them.

In the membership count alone, AMC has had 911 persons join since 1960. Beyond the membership numbers, AMC is a *virtual* congregation to an estimated 650 persons. This number includes all listed members, associate members, people who attend worship with some regularity, children, and relatives/friends of people associated with AMC. The church is a resource for some community persons who are served through our mission groups. Our pastors are sometimes called on to serve this expanded congregation. It is apparent that AMC's influence reaches beyond the parameters of its membership list.

It is hard to know what to make of the uneven attendance patterns, especially among our members. Where are they when they aren't at AMC on a given Sunday morning? It is known that some regularly attend other churches but haven't transferred their membership. At any given time, about thirty of our young members are attending colleges away from Akron. However, some young adult members who live in this community rarely attend services at AMC and haven't transferred their memberships to other churches.

Some of our members are absent from worship because of travel requirements connected with their jobs. A small number have to work on Sunday. Others are home because of sickness or to take care of a family member. A few serve on regional or national boards that sometimes meet over the weekends.

As is the case for the wider church, membership and church attendance aren't taken as seriously as they once were. In years past, many of us went to church every Sunday unless sickness or weather prevented it. We even attended Sunday evening services and other church events during the week. But those days would seem to be gone. Being in church on Sunday doesn't seem to mean what it once did.

But, does it really matter if fewer of us come to church regularly? While some of us may experience angst over attendance numbers, AMC has historically been ambivalent about becoming too large. So, if it is our wish to remain small, maybe we aren't bothered as much when attendance lags. The resistance to largeness was evident in the earliest records of our congregation. Then, we believed that if we grew too large we would lose our closeness and mutual accountability. It is a truism that the larger a group becomes, the less possible it is to maintain relationships.

Indeed, managing church growth has always been an explicit goal at AMC. Over the years AMC has intentionally studied the issue of growth. Within a span of three years during the 1970s, three separate studies on church growth were presented to the congregation. These studies found both theological and practical reasons for containing church size. Each of the studies emphasized planting new churches as an alternative to expansion at AMC.

Thus, in 1975 we launched a group of six couples to the Elizabethtown area where some of our members lived. They called themselves the Donegal Fellowship. Unfortunately, the group didn't grow significantly and disbanded after about three years. Two of the couples returned to AMC. Some of the Donegal group felt it failed because there wasn't pastoral oversight soon enough. Others believed that their children's needs weren't being met. Perhaps reflecting the spirit of the times and the ages of the members, the group was ambivalent about being too traditional in its expression of spirituality. It appears that the group didn't have enough positive shared values to hold it together.

A second group of about nine adults and five children left AMC in 1977 to establish what would become the Pilgrims Mennonite Church. They met in several locations until they settled on rented space in the MCC Welcoming Place. Now about 80 adults and children assemble for worship each week at PMC. They have a part-time pastor. The congregation never intended to become large. Their growth has been steady but measured. Early in their history, they joined the Lancaster Mennonite Conference.

A third group, consisting of 26 members and their children, left Akron in 1985 to establish Community Mennonite Church of Lancaster, a church in inner city Lancaster. They chose that site to accommodate members—and potential members—who lived in or near Lancaster. They were intentional about wanting to be an urban presence. About 250 people now worship at CMCL.

The members at CMCL joined the Atlantic Coast Mennonite Conference, which was a part of the Mennonite Church, and they also chose to affiliate with the General Conference Mennonite Church. Since the merger of the two main Mennonite bodies, they remain only with ACC, which connects them organically with the Mennonite Church USA. They have a full-time pastor, a three-fourths time associate pastor, and a half-time director of children and youth. Because their church building can't be expanded, the group has two worship services to accommodate the attenders. Their growth has been significant.

One very important dynamic in the demography of AMC is that we are not an *ancestral* congregation. Most of us weren't born into AMC and many of our extended families live elsewhere. We have no *family benches* as the churches did where some of us came from. Thus, the genetic glue that can bind congregations together is hardly

Community Mennonite Church, Lancaster, Pa., 2008.

present at AMC. We have many people in attendance from two-generation households and a few from three generations. However, we have no four-generation households. Only one marriage of AMC's adult children—who both grew up in this church—has occurred in our 50-year history.

The children of AMC tend not to come back when they leave for college or service. It is most likely that careers, marriage to spouses from other parts of the country, adventure, and simply not wanting to be in their parents' church might explain why they don't come back.

In general, when people stop attending AMC it is hard to know *why* they leave or even *where* they go. While we have public ceremonies for people coming *into* the church, little is said or known about those who *leave*. We do have public blessings for members who depart for service assignments or for employment in other communities.

Generally, the people who leave through *the side door* don't tell us where they have gone or why they left. While we may temporarily grieve their loss, few of us reach out to them. Most of the time we don't know where they have gone. Maybe out of sight is out of mind. In an era of weakened interpersonal attachments, people can come and go in church life without being noticed. This trend has become more common at AMC and elsewhere.

A recent factor limiting the number of *new members* coming *into* AMC is that we are not as uniquely positioned as we once were in our Mennonite community. In an earlier time, we stood out distinctively from the other churches. We were known as a comfortable place for people seeking refuge from their conservative home churches. Now many of those churches are very similar to AMC. At one point AMC was one of just a few Mennonite churches in the area that would accept persons who were divorced and remarried. Many of these couples can now find acceptance elsewhere.

A second factor that impacts AMC's growth is the presence of neighboring mega churches. Some people who would be potential members at Akron are attracted to the high energy, contemporary worship services in these churches. This atmosphere seems to represent a new and authentic form of Christianity to these people. Even smaller churches in the community have worship teams, coffee bars, and other nontraditional kinds of worship. This style of Christianity is simple, positive and dynamic in contrast to the more formal and intellectual spirit at AMC.

On the other hand, AMC is still attractive to prospective members who are theologically and politically progressive. Our peace and justice theme is a beacon to them. They are also drawn to an environment that welcomes questions and resists easy answers. The AMC position on women in leadership, especially from the early 1970s on, has also been a positive factor in attracting new members. Perhaps because of our relationship to MCC, many of our members have a broad worldview and an expanded awareness of global needs. This attracts a certain kind of person to AMC. It has been our niche for many years. However, as more Mennonite churches in our community become *global* in vision, we are becoming one of many options available to prospective members. Even some new MCC workers are attending worship in other churches while in the past AMC was more commonly chosen.

One negative factor affecting our growth—especially for younger people—is our aging demographic. We have a large segment of older members and a relatively smaller number of younger adults. Our baby boomers are now approaching retirement and they aren't being replaced by an equal number of younger adults. This can influence whether prospective young members—especially those with children—choose to attend. At the same time this factor can also weaken the commitment present young members have for *remaining* at AMC.

When we started our church 50 years ago, we were predominantly young. Now we are predominantly a graying congregation. In the beginning, we had three members 65 or older. They represented only about four percent of the group. Now we have 132 senior members. Most attend regularly. Today with our average attendance of 270, it is estimated that about one third of the worshippers are over 65.

When we compare our profile with that of the American population and the broader Mennonite church, the percentage of our congregation that is over sixty-five is expanding more rapidly than either of these groups. A Mennonite Church USA survey indicates that from 1972 to 2006 the number of members under age 45 in the broader church has gone from 54 percent to 30 percent. Using a slightly different age cohort, the number of AMCers less than age 50 has declined from 69 percent in 1983 to 29 percent today. Of

Ura and Gladys Gingerich, 1986.

special concern is the fact that there are only 19 persons at AMC in the 40 to 44 year age group to take the place of 40 people in the 45 to 49 year age group. That suggests that the group we will turn to for continued leadership and financial support is becoming much smaller.

However, any church is about more than numbers. It is much more about people. That is certainly true at AMC. Throughout our history we have been a treasure trove of unusually gifted people. What has strengthened our church is that we are a blend of persons from many different places, different personalities, varied careers, and even some diversity of beliefs. At the core, we share a common commitment to the centrality of Christ in our lives and in our church. And we stay remarkably loyal to core Anabaptist beliefs. We are frequently reminded of one of the central beliefs—peace and justice.

We are authors, scientists, professors, accomplished musicians, physicians, nurses, medical workers, information technologists, business persons, administrators, sales people, office workers, hoof trimmers, mothers, fathers, grandparents, athletes, teachers, dairy specialists, church agency leaders, skilled builders and persons skilled in various crafts. We have done seminal research on the health of the Great Lakes, the Chesapeake Bay, helped establish the NASA observatory on Mauna Kea in Hawaii. We have served on the Boards of international agencies. We have participated in some significant international diplomacy and have headed numerous church and secular agencies.

Even though we have little racial or ethnic diversity, we have a commendable sensitivity to the needs of minorities both nationally and locally. Our parking lot has more Chevys and Toyotas than Mercedes. We are committed to simple living. It is rather remarkable that the character of our founders has lived on with very little substantive change in those of us who are keeping their dreams alive. The pilgrims now on the journey look strikingly similar to the ones who sat next to the fire trucks in Brownstown so many years ago! We would appear to be on the same path. That path is where we continue our journey.

Chapter Three

Governing
Pilgrims

"NO GROUP CAN PERSIST FOR ANY APPRECIABLE TIME WITH-
OUT DEVELOPING SOME PATTERNS OF LEADERSHIP, SOME DIF-
FERENTIATION OF ROLES AMONG ITS MEMBERS, SOME MEANS OF
MANAGING CONFLICT, SOME WAYS OF ARTICULATING SHARED
VALUES AND NORMS, AND SOME SANCTIONS TO ASSURE AC-
CEPTABLE LEVELS OF CONFORMITY TO THOSE NORMS."

MEEKS (P.111)

E ven Pilgrims need to *govern* and *be governed*. All of us do better when we have direction from our leaders. Individually we
often fail at self-governance. While over governance can stifle creativity,
groups that have too little direction tend to disintegrate. Ultimately,
governance originates with God and leaders are called to carry out God's
purposes. In his role as leader, Moses guided the Children of Israel out
of captivity. With God as his Enabler, Moses led "his congregation" on
their route. He settled disputes among his people and played a very
important part in recording and disseminating the most historic Judeo-
Christian document of governance—the Ten Commandments.

The Apostle Paul was God's servant in giving direction to the
early church. In his letters to the expanding church he cajoled, plead-
ed, scolded and governed. Although in announcing that in Christ *all*

things are new, he was not timid in proscribing what this new freedom would mean. Part pastor and part social worker, he advised Christians about their responsibility to take care of their parents and the poor, how to honor marriage, and how to live as moral beings. Theologian Wayne Meeks states that Paul's visits to the various Christian communities and his epistles were "the means of more direct and specific attempts at social control."

However, Paul didn't impose a hierarchical pattern of governance on his people. In I Peter 2:5, he called on all members to become a *holy priesthood,* suggesting that governance was to be shared. During the Reformation, Martin Luther spoke about the *priesthood of all believers.* From our beginning as Anabaptists, we also applied that concept to the way we viewed governance. We embraced the belief in *servant leadership* that was to be exercised *in the name of Christ.* These concepts of governance still influence us at AMC today.

Menno Simons and other contemporary leaders played a very important role in guiding this growing and persecuted radical wing of the Protestant Reformation. While they recognized God as their ultimate governor and took counsel from the community, they were its leaders. They wrote and signed the Schleitheim and the Dordrecht confessions and used them as instruments to govern the community.

When our charter members left Monterey, we didn't have a governance vacuum very long. Indeed, even before our first worship service in the fire hall, the process for self-governance had already begun. A committee of leaders had been meeting in the months before the move to Brownstown to decide, among other things, where the group would meet, who would serve as temporary pastor and how the church bills would be paid. These governors would continue to serve as an *Advisory Committee* for a number of years. This committee consisted of five men.

The church elected its first female governor, Kathy Hostetler, in 1963. Her husband John noted that on the evening of this landmark event, both he and the new governor were not able "to calm down and get a good night of sleep" until they were at peace with their decision.

Even though female leadership was uncommon in the broader church at that time, she was welcomed as a voting member of the Advisory Committee. She was recruited, in part, for her secretarial skills. At the congregational meeting to confirm her appointment, there was considerable deliberation but clear support for her.

John and Kathy Hostetler, 2003.

In the early years of AMC, the group was small enough to allow governance to take place at its weekly Wednesday night meeting. The frequency and intimacy of those meetings kept the gap between the governors and the governed very small. The congregation had doubled in size to 92 members by 1963. Some aspects of governance were then assigned to the newly formed house church groups. However, final decisions would still be made in all-members monthly business meetings. These changes indicate that governance patterns were adjusting to meet the needs of a growing church.

By 1968, with the membership at 163 and the governance becoming more complex, AMC adopted a more *bureaucratic* structure. Pastor Kermit Derstine created a flow chart complete with lines and boxes. It identified who was responsible to whom. The congregation was divided into areas of service that included Pastoral Care and Congregational Life, Preaching and Worship, Congregational Mission, Resources and Administration, and Education.

The chairpersons of these committees, identified as elders, formed the Advisory Council. The Council was given increased responsibility for governing the congregation, although house church groups maintained some responsibility for discussing matters of concern. The Council, however, brought all of the big decisions to the monthly business meeting of the congregation for further discussion and action. Among other things, the congregation developed the *Discipline Standard* as a method of governance. (see appendix) That step was timely because AMC was soon confronted with the need to deal with the first marital separation of a member couple.

As with most organizational structures, AMC continued to morph into different configurations. During the 1970s and until the mid 1980s, the Council was comprised of the chairs of the various congregational ministries plus the officers of Council. The Council members were governors *with* portfolios. That is, they were on Council as representatives of the departments they chaired. While they participated in broader discussions confronting the church, these Council members clearly were there on behalf of their departments.

As the membership of AMC grew from 180 members in 1970 to 345 in 1985, so did its programs. During that time the organizational chart expanded dramatically. We were becoming a complex social organization. To deal with that complexity the main governing body, the Advisory Council, underwent a major change in 1985 and was renamed Congregational Council.

At that time, a task force recommended moving away from portfolio-based Council to a group that was more representative of—and responsive to—the congregation. There was some feeling within the congregation that Council was making decisions that didn't always reflect the best interests of the members. The initial proposal was for house church groups to choose Council members from among their group. However, this plan was modified because there were 26 house church groups, and that would have made Council too large. Ultimately, the new system that chose representatives from a *cluster* of house churches turned out to be cumbersome and became unworkable.

After a number of years, the Leadership Coordinating Committee (LCC) who chose people for other congregational positions

Congregational Council: Herman Bontrager, chair, 1985.

began selecting Council members. The LCC has attempted to recruit members who reflect the demographics of the congregation. Council members serve *without portfolio* with the exception of the treasurer whose appointment is automatic. An executive committee, consisting of the Chair, Vice Chair and a third Council member, is active between meetings to conduct the urgent business of the congregation. The Chair also supervises the pastors and is the *de facto* chief executive officer of the congregation.

There are 33 committees that carry out the work of the congregation. They serve under the Commissions of Administration, Worship and Care, Resource, Education, and Outreach. About one-half of the active members of AMC participate in ongoing church assignments. Some volunteer on their own to serve on committees, but most are selected by the LCC. All positions are affirmed by a congregational vote. Their typical terms are for three years. To the degree that these workers have governing functions, it would indicate that a significant number of members help shape congregational life.

Throughout our 50-year history, it has been hard to know how to best conduct the business of AMC. Obviously, when the membership was small, the meetings could be more informal and most members were able to participate in the governance. As we grew and matters became more complex, we began to conduct the congregational meetings by Robert's Rules of Order to assure that decisions were properly made and understood.

In the mid 1980s, we substituted a consensus model that set aside the formality of motions, seconds and votes. It was incumbent upon the Chair to get a sense of the group before moving forward with governance. The results were varied but the change did little to increase attendance or the ownership of decisions. We currently conduct important votes by ballot, usually requiring a two-thirds majority for passage.

Other attempts had been made to improve the governance processes at AMC. The Congregational Chair made a rather dramatic

Discernment Sunday: Lila Garber, Urbane Peachey, Anna Mae Voth, and Don Mellinger, 1998.

change in the format of the congregational meetings in 1997. The meetings were reframed as *Discernment Sunday* and the time of the meetings was moved from Sunday evening to the Sunday School hour. For a while the meeting was followed by a fellowship meal. Decision-making was to be experienced as a celebration of community. While part of that format has survived and attendance is slightly better; nevertheless, only a minority of the congregation attends.

In January 2008, the Congregational Council convened a Vision Retreat to review a number of important AMC issues including

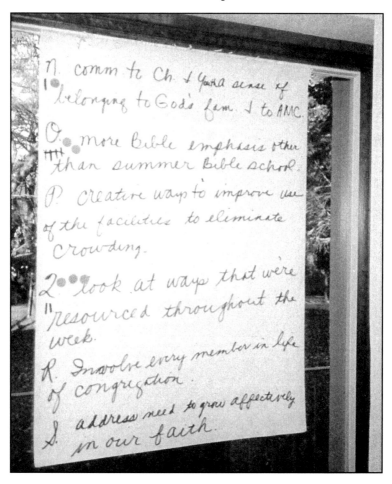

Poster notes from a retreat, 1983.

governance. The retreat was held in the Fellowship Hall from Friday evening through Saturday afternoon. In contrast to some past retreats in which only selected leaders of the congregation were invited, this time all the AMC members/attenders were welcomed. Approximately 60 persons plus Council members attended the retreat.

A considerable amount of time was spent discussing the strengths of the congregation using the Appreciative Inquiry Model as a guiding instrument. Although many strong points at AMC were identified, the participants also identified some areas for growth. Among other ideas, they suggested that Council find ways to connect more closely with the congregation on matters of governance. Responding to that recommendation, the Council assigned each Council member to 14 households to facilitate better two-way communications. The results of this effort have been mixed. Some AMC members have responded to the updates with either affirmation or suggestions. However, most have not.

Except for the first few years in our history, one of the main impediments to good governance has been the apparent disinterest in decision making by many members. Some would appear to care little about what the Council does. In addition, the small numbers of members who attend Discernment meetings may simply reflect disinterest. Perhaps it shows that they are at peace with the way the church is governed. It may also reflect the reduced importance some people place on connecting closely with church. What is known is that some members who don't attend Discernment meetings have strong opinions about governance issues but either share them only with friends or harbor them privately.

Reflecting on the history of governance at AMC, it would appear that the effectiveness of the Council has been limited by the short terms of its councilors. Typically, a councilor serves only one three-year term. While it is possible for them to serve longer, it rarely happens. Obviously, the first year on Council tends to be spent becoming oriented to the task of governing. By the time Council members enter their third year, some will be moving psychologically toward the finish line, especially if they feel their time on Council hasn't been meaningful. Perhaps ways need to be found to make the experience better for all council members. It is important for everyone to be fully engaged throughout their three-year terms. It would also appear to be beneficial for their terms to be longer.

One of the effects of the rapid turnover is that Council can lose institutional memory. Current governors often don't know what previous Councils have decided. The archival record of this congregation reveals significant failures in the follow-up to previous decisions or the reintroduction of issues that had been processed before. The ongoing need for adequate space for the programs of the church is a good example. Also, our tendency to make up our budget shortfalls in the last month of the year can take newer members by surprise and can lead to lengthy discussions. Longer terms could be very helpful in producing continuity and quality in decision-making at AMC. Extending the officers' terms could also be helpful.

Over the years, we have had good intentions in the ways we have chosen to govern AMC. As modern Anabaptists, we don't like hierarchical styles of governance. We resist giving too much authority to leaders who are set apart from the people in the benches. *Gelassenheit* has ruled! Although many of us don't attend congregational meetings or serve on Council, most of us *do care* about what happens at AMC. Thus, we will need to continue to look for ways to involve more of us in the decision-making process.

Given the failure of past attempts to involve more members in decision-making, we need to commission and bless our governing body—Congregational Council—to act on our behalf. We also need to continue to invite good people to serve on Council—and for longer terms. Pilgrims need to *govern* and to *be governed.* The very health of the church depends on doing it right.

Chapter Four

Mutually Affectionate Pilgrims

The Apostle Paul, when addressing an earlier group of pilgrims in Rome, encouraged them to "love one another with mutual affection." *Romans 12:10 (nrsv).* Eugene Peterson paraphrases this same passage in *The Message*—"Be good friends who love deeply . . ." *The Bible Commentary* (edited by F.F. Bruce) says Paul was recommending "touches of affectionate tenderness."

Paul's ecclesiology made close, affectionate relationships a central theme for the early church. Although church was about worshipping God, learning scripture, and shaping moral behavior, it is clear that it was also about relationship building. Paul wanted the people in the early churches to form friendships that would provide both spiritual and emotional support. It is no accident that Paul used the terms *sister* and *brother* to describe the relationships that he expected members to have.

How close does our theology of church fit the Pauline model? In our fifty-year history, have we been brothers and sisters to each other? Is AMC the primary group to which we belong and where we get our support? Do we notice when a fellow member has been absent from church? If we felt that kind of closeness in our early years at AMC, has it weakened since then? Or, in the pluralistic world that we are now a part of, has the Pauline model for the church gone out of style?

If merely being together leads to emotional closeness, we should be doing well. On average, about 270 of us gather for worship each Sunday. In addition, many of us are members of house church groups. In that setting we are able to bond with at least a small sector of the congregation. Discipleship Hour classes regularly bring us into contact with each other. In terms of church activities, the schedule has been packed full of things to do with each other for years. But do these activities themselves create mutually affectionate pilgrims who love deeply?

Already in the first decade of AMC we were concerned with losing our closeness. Noting the impact that numerical growth was bringing, Pastor Derstine lamented, "We are on a flat spot." He believed that the rapid growth was interfering with our level of intimacy, even though many of us were involved in house church groups.

Despite that concern, we kept on growing. We didn't want to put up a *no vacancy* sign by the church. That growth meant that we would need more space to meet our spiritual, educational—and *social needs*. Even though we dragged our feet every time a building program was discussed, we went ahead with the expansion. We always pushed these concerns about growth aside and added on to the building, perhaps believing we would find ways to meet our needs in our newer, expanded space.

However, for the first time in our history, we rejected a building plan in 2006. Although a majority of the members who voted favored the plan, the total vote didn't meet the two-thirds level required by AMC polity. Was the reason for the defeat about money and simplicity or was it about resisting getting too large and having growth push us even farther away from each other? Were there other reasons?

Indeed, steady membership growth over the years has made it hard to maintain intimate connections. Now, at the worship service, we may not know the person sitting on the bench next to us. What sociologists refer to as *anomie*—literally, being nameless—takes on special meaning. It is hard to be affectionate with people whose names we don't even know. We may be sitting alongside a person whom we consider to be a visitor only to learn that he or she has been attending AMC regularly.

But size isn't the only factor restricting our closeness. For some of us church is no longer as central to our lives as it once was. It is but one of many activities in our schedule. We have other groups to which we belong that can give us a feeling of belonging. The meaning of membership and attendance is less important to us than it once was. In our earlier history, we might have felt guilty for missing church, but that is no longer an influence for many of us. If legalism drove us to church in the past, it certainly doesn't anymore.

The choice that some of us make to push church to the margins creates an outcome that is predictable. That is, the less contact we have with church friends, the less affection we will feel for each other. Group cohesion is directly affected by propinquity. If we aren't physically near to each other frequently, we tend to lose our closeness.

Is it possible that AMC is also influenced by the *packed suitcase* factor? We are a people on the move. We have come from many places and from different backgrounds, and we travel a great deal. Some of us are gone for a while on service assignments. AMC is a temporary stopping-off place for some of us. It is hard for a church that has many people who are here for a short time or part time, to connect deeply with each other. It is especially hard for newcomers to make connections within a fluid congregation. While this in/outflow is enriching it can also inhibit social bonding. We tend to attach less to each other when there is a significant amount of tentativeness in our relationships.

This issue has been with us for a long time. However, only recently have we begun to name it and to identify it as a theological and strategic issue. In a congregational vision retreat held in January 2008, more than 70 people in attendance identified it as a primary need at AMC. They seemed to be asking for what the French call *esprit de corps*—an increase in the closeness and affection that we need within the larger congregation.

However, we do have our places where relationships can be formed. Not surprisingly the most meaningful relationships are often formed in our **house church** groups. They have been a part of AMC from early in our history. Pastor Derstine established them because of his concern that we need to be accountable to each other in order to remain close. Members were expected to join. Although participation has waxed and waned over the years, house church remains a vital part of connecting at AMC. These assemblies of six to twelve people who gather in each other's homes have been a connecting point for many people over the years. Lifelong friendships have come from these groups. This is especially notable in the group of oldest members who have been together for most of their history at Akron. They have stood by each other through major illnesses and deaths. Indeed, house churches do supplement the larger church in meeting the needs of members.

House church 6: left to right: Dale Hershey, Megan Yoder, Dwight Yoder, Herman Bontrager, Zachary Yoder, Barb Penner, Julie Yoder, Dot Hershey, and Jeanette Bontrager, 2005.

Most of the house church groups express their bond with each other by bringing meals to sick members, assisting with house repairs, and by giving spiritual and emotional support to members. Sometimes the support is expressed through giving materially to each other. Recently, Brian Weaver—then unemployed and as a volunteer—did significant remodeling of a house into which one of his house church members was moving.

The low point for participation in house church groups was 1994 when only 40 percent of AMCers belonged to a group. Today, with renewed emphasis, 197 people or 60 percent belong to one of the 22 house church groups. Persons who don't belong can find it more difficult to connect with other members.

Another attempt to establish closeness has been through **fellowship meals.** Although, in our early years these meals were served monthly, they are now served three times a year. This brings together 100 to 150 persons to each meal. Just as with house church, only about half of the people participate. Perhaps fewer come because of limited space in the fellowship room. Only about 150 to 200 fit into the room. At the upper end of that number, the diners are crowded and the room is noisy. Tables are so closely placed that it is hard to move through the room, especially for older members whose mobility is restricted. Because of noise, diners often are restricted in their conversations to the few people next to them. The inadequate fellowship room is a strategic issue that remains unresolved. However, the event is meaningful to many people.

In 1998 Pastor Peachey initiated a light lunch, **Sunday Soup,** as a way of welcoming temporary service workers at MCC and other visitors. Somewhat to his surprise, regular members began to come as well. Perhaps they were seeking more connections with others. This gathering has been especially appealing to young families as an alternative to going out to restaurants or cooking at home. At times, up to 150 people attend Sunday Soup, which is now served four times per year.

Fellowship Meal: Ethel Shank, Kendall and Ron Hunsicker, Anita Brendle, Paul Ruth, and Deb and Jennae Havner, 1998.

Christmas Tea, left to right: Kaylor Rosenberry, Julia Yoder, Annie Wise, and Barbara Weaver, 2007.

*Christmas
Program Tea:
Esther Hostetter,
Chris Hostetter,
Lloyd and Goldie
Kuhns, and Irma
Bowman, 1996.*

*AMC Summer Picnic:
Rich Crockett, 1997.*

An annual **summer picnic** was started in 1960 and was held for a brief time at Long's Park in Lancaster, then transferred to Woodcrest Retreat in Ephrata. It found a permanent home at Akron's Roland Park in 1964 and ran continuously until 2007. In the early years multigenerational softball games brought excitement and hilarity as well as some sore bodies. Jim Hallman sought some revenge against AMC youth who were heckling him by sending a foul ball in their direction. Coach Ruth Wenger used the occasion to scout out future field hockey players from among the AMC girls at the picnic. Conversations at the table lasted long after the food was all gone. Attendance had dwindled and it was difficult to get enough volunteers to staff it. In the peak years, games and sporting events were planned and the Lion's Club Pavilion was filled. Some members recall that it was a joyful time to gather as a church family. It has been rescheduled for the summer of 2009.

Coffee Hour also has a long history at AMC. It was begun in 1972 and has continued uninterrupted since that time. It has traditionally been scheduled between the worship service and the Discipleship Hour. For a brief time it was moved to the end of the morning schedule, but devout sippers lobbied to return it to the traditional time. Their wishes were granted. Throughout its history, Coffee Hour has been well supported. Participants gather enthusiastically in the foyer and in the Assembly Room for conversation and a boost.

Coffee Hour: Don and Priscilla Ziegler, 2001.

People who prefer a more intimate and peaceful setting are encouraged to meet in the prayer room. Not surprisingly, some people who attend AMC find the Coffee Hour quite intimidating because of the crowdedness in the foyer or from not being comfortable in informal conversations. For them, the Coffee Hour is not appealing.

Some of the people who enjoy Coffee Hour find it difficult to end their time together and choose not to attend a Discipleship Hour group. Their revelry can interfere with classes that are held nearby.

WMSC sewing group: Kathleen Moyer and Kathy Hostetler, 1981.

Mennonite Women's Retreat: Esther Hostetter, Zem Martin, Grace Brubaker, Jean Miller, Jeanette Bontrager, and Karen Alderfer, 1998.

Quilting at Material Resources Center, Ephrata: Kathy Hostetler, Louise Leatherman, Ruth Detweiler, and Helena Dueck, 2001.

Tensions have arisen between the Coffee Hour people and the Discipleship Hour people. But if there is one connecting event that many people want to preserve in its present format, it is the Coffee Hour! This ritual does, indeed, reflect the Anabaptist value of community. It is the one time during the week that the participants are able to have a less-scripted relationship with each other. To keep the moment even more Anabaptist, the group has opted to serve only fair trade coffee and tea. Because this coffee is more expensive, coffee drinkers have been asked to make voluntary contributions to the cause.

The **Women's Missionary and Service Commission** was begun at AMC in 1963 and was important to the women and girls of the congregation. It morphed into **Mennonite Women**, following a similar change in the national Women's Missionary and Service Commission. In its earlier version it sponsored an annual mother/daughter banquet. However, in 1987 it was changed to Women's Spring Banquet out of sensitivity to single women or women without children. In the beginning, monthly meetings were held for service projects, including sewing various items for MCC. Presently they plan a one-day spring retreat and prepare the care packages for college students.

Retreats are an exciting part of the history of AMC. The richness of seeing each other in a different setting that was more relaxed and informal has been difficult to replace. The conversations that people had on walks, under shade trees or on canoe rides was a vital part of church life then. The first all-church retreat was held in 1970 at the Black Rock Camp in southern Lancaster County. About a dozen more were scheduled at various other locations, including at Messiah College. The last all-church retreat was in 1992.

Most were well attended and some of them were quite sophisticated in format. The planners brought in outside speakers, and had workshops and talent shows. People attending were enthusiastic, especially the young people. However, the all-church retreats were discontinued, in part, because of costs. Several marriage enrichment retreats

Church Retreat: Louise and Warren Leatherman, and Esther and Albert Miller, 1977.

AMC Retreat: Bob Wyble, Janet Weber, and Sam Wenger, 1986.

AMC Retreat: Gerry Horst and Chet Raber, 1986.

Women's Retreat: Marlene Kaufman, presenter, 1998.

were also a part of our history. More recently, gender-specific retreats have been held.

AMC has been moving toward more specialized activities. A **Men's Breakfast** is now scheduled monthly at a nearby restaurant. Some women gather for an evening **Bible Study.** Young mothers have a **Moms Meeting** every other week. Since 1996 the **55+ers** have been meeting four times per year for a light meal and a program. The **Lunch Bunch**, a group of 10 to 12 single/widowed women, has been enjoying monthly fellowship for over 12 years. The **bicyclists** at AMC make frequent treks to both nearby and more distant locations. Perhaps owing to congregational size and our demographics, we are clustering in smaller groups in order to connect with at least a part of the congregation.

AMC has a rich history of **musical and stage performances.** As early as 1966 our thespians combined with others from Monterey

AMC biking group. Seated on steps from left to right: Merle Gingerich, Carla Neufeld, Dennis Clemmer, Fern Clemmer, Linda Frey, Rick Haller, Deb Brennaman, Rod Houser, and Don Ziegler; standing in rear, Ron Flickinger (3 others in rear unidentified), 1980.

MYF Christmas Pageant: Sarah Roth, Jenna Garber, Corin Kidwell, Matt Harms, Michael Kuhns, and Heidi Horst (Daniel), 1997.

Mennonite to produce *Christ in the Concrete City*. During the 1980s we performed *Godspell, Cotton Patch Gospel,* and *Amahl and the Night Visitor.* These talents—all the way from stagehands through the directors and performers—produced entertainment that enriched us all.

When Don Brunk and his sister Cathy proposed staging *Godspell* at AMC, there was some doubt about whether we could—or even *should* do it. But with the help of Chris Hostetter providing support and encouragement, it was accomplished. Flo Harnish later directed *Amahl* to sold-out houses. These productions might not have made it to Broadway, but we were pleased with their efforts.

And we have had some very significant individual performances. Who can ever forget the rich baritone voice of former member Tony Brown, who went on to sing professionally, or the wonderful soprano voice of our own Kristin Sims, whose name graces the programs of local professional productions in opera and sacred concerts?

AMC 40th Anniversary Concert: Cheryl Faul Gingerich and Tony Brown, 1999.

We have also been blessed with the singing of people like Ruth Ann Kulp, Merle Gingerich and others. Some of our instrumentalists have performed professionally—some at national venues.

The choirs from AMC and Neffsville Mennonite Church combined to perform Vivaldi's *Gloria*. For several years, the choirs from Neffsville, Bethel, Monterey and Akron joined to sing at Palm Sunday evening services. Many other outstanding performances, including some done by our children, have taken place over the years. However, most of these creative activities took place several decades ago, and nothing at this level has taken place since. Was there a *golden age* that may be hard to repeat?

Perhaps the *most* connecting of all the activities are those done by and for the **MYF** (Mennonite Youth Fellowship). Their youthful energy and delightful impiety have regularly brought us out of our safe predictability. While we are happy to contribute money to their worthwhile causes, we are also glad to be entertained by what the youth bring us, especially when they ask us to come in costume and out of our more scripted roles. Some of us have found remnants from the closet or the attic to bring color to the events, including short skirts and leisure suits from the 70s. It is one event where we can *clap with both hands* and maybe even act a bit silly, if but for the moment.

Various fund raising events are held each year to support the trips to the Youth Convention as well as their service ventures. The MYF sells subs, baked potatoes, and desserts for the fellowship meals. They also have had cookie bakes, created an AMC cookbook, and offered their labors for baby-sitting, yard raking, and many other things. Most of these activities are fundraisers, although some are service projects. Perhaps, more importantly, they are ways for members to connect with the youth and with each other. The congregation also has special ceremonies for MYFers when they graduate from high school, and we continue to remember them by sending *care packages* when they are away at college.

The two main social/connecting events that have survived for several decades are the **pig roast/auction** and the **spaghetti supper**. Pig roasting *connoisseur* Elvin Stoltzfus has become an irreplaceable fixture in providing some of the best pork on earth. His efforts make the whole event come to life. The food and the auction that follows are responsible for raising money for the MYF activities and the *scholarship fund*. The fund subsidizes tuition costs for AMC students attending Anabaptist colleges and universities.

Auctioneer Ken Martin, from a neighboring Brethren in Christ church, has donated his time for many years. His ability to extract unbelievable amounts of money from the back pockets of the attenders is remarkable. It helps that his standup comedy routine, assisted by Gerry Horst, weakens our will power. These gatherings are well attended and filled with humor and enthusiasm. These excesses lead to good seats at Phillies ballgames and gourmet meals on the decks of the gourmands among us. In the chaos of auctions, we perform differently. Usually that

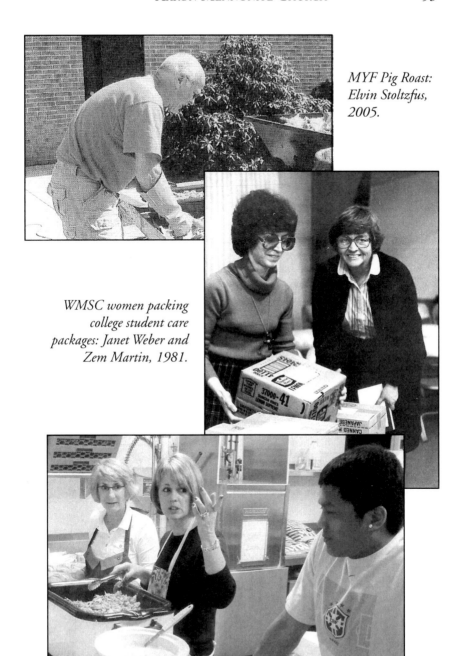

MYF Pig Roast: Elvin Stoltzfus, 2005.

WMSC women packing college student care packages: Janet Weber and Zem Martin, 1981.

MYF Pig Roast/Auction: Delores Nolt, Linda Horst, and Noah Passage, 2009.

*MYF Spaghetti Supper:
Glenn Weaver and
Dale Huber, 1981.*

*MYF Auction:
Heather Horst, Rita
McCrae (Boer), and
Ken Martin, 2000.*

MYF Auction sale items, 2000.

means *better*. At their other event, the spaghetti supper, the MYFers serve the food in a more formal banquet style and often prepare skits and games that involve the audience. It also is a joyful church family event.

At a less visible level, individual connecting goes on at AMC through the various **mentoring** programs. This gives adults an opportunity to relate in a meaningful way with children and youth. Some of these mentoring relationships have developed into long-term friendships. In addition, these relationships take place within the MYF (Life Planning), Junior MYF (Life Quest), and in Venture Club and Share a Life programs for younger children. These programs have made church more meaningful

Venture Club Talent and Hobby Night: Eli Passage with his stamp collection, 1999.

Share a Life: Sheryl Krafft and Marcia Hartzler, 1998.

for AMC children and youth as well as their adult partners. Many mentors attend the concerts or ballgames of the youth and children. Some comfort them during tough times. The numerous ways adults connect with young people in our church are impressive.

Are we connecting enough? Are we affectionate in the way Paul challenged the Romans to be? We certainly provide many opportunities for members to connect through various activities. And many of us connect meaningfully in other spontaneous ways. Indeed, we have a long history of very enriching activities. AMC has been an exciting, creative place to be with our friends.

However, we are becoming busier and are finding it harder to staff and participate in some of the programs that have been a part of our history. Because of that reality, it is especially important that we continue to find new activities that are meaningful to each generation. Traditions can be important, but only if they are carried out with energy, passion, and emotion. Activities alone are not enough. We need to create new ways of being intimate with each other and at deeper levels. We want to be *friends who love deeply.* That is a real measure of a congregation.

Chapter Five

Pilgrims' Place of Worship

JESUS VALUED SACRED BUILDINGS. WHEN HE ENCOUNTERED THE MERCHANTS USING THE TEMPLE AS A PLACE TO DO BUSI- NESS HE, IN AN ACT OF ANGER, UPSET THEIR TABLES AND ASKED THEM, "IS IT NOT WRITTEN, 'MY HOUSE SHALL BE CALLED A HOUSE OF PRAYER FOR ALL THE NATIONS'? BUT YOU HAVE MADE IT A DEN OF ROBBERS."

MARK 11: 17(NRSV)

The buildings in which we worship reflect the values, personality and circumstances of the members. Monterey, our mother church, chose an old vacant church building as their first place of worship. AMC used a fire hall for three-and-a-half years. These were humble beginnings, but not surprising for a pilgrim people. If we need any reminders of the simplicity motif in our church buildings, we only need to sing the first hymn in our *Worship Book*. It asks the question, "What is this place where we are meeting?" And answers, "Only a house, the earth its floor, walls and a roof sheltering people, windows for light, an open door." It concludes that church is about God and people more than buildings.

On the other hand, the significant role that buildings have played for God's people has a long history. In the Old Testament, the temple building was essential to God's people. It was where the Torah was secured, where teaching took place, and where various ceremonies were practiced. Perhaps most of all, the temple was where God's people gathered. Temples were often ornate, elaborate and expensive. When temples were destroyed, great effort was put into rebuilding them. Thousands of years after the Second Temple was destroyed in Jerusalem worshippers still gather at its one remaining wall to wail and to pray. In the above passage quoted from Mark, it is clear that Jesus valued the place of the temple in religious life. He acknowledged the central role it played for God's people. Jesus attended Passover services and used the temple for teaching.

First century Christians had no temples or other identifiable edifices of their own. In Acts 19:9-10, it is noted that the Apostle Paul abandoned teaching in the temple in Ephesus because of stubborn unbelievers and relocated to the Hall of Tyrannus for two years. The Hall served as a place of leisure for people in the community. It included a gymnasium where Paul presented his lectures while the Hall members were resting elsewhere.

For the most part, however, the early Christians met in each other's homes. Author Robert Wright says, "Borrowed homes and meeting halls were the initial infrastructure" for the early church. That pattern continued for several centuries. At first, house churches were formed for mutual support during times of persecution. They later served as communities of teaching and discernment. As Christians became more accepted in the broader culture, they gathered in larger groups. That meant they would need more spacious buildings.

However, according to L. Michael White, "There were as yet no church buildings. At this stage the house church was primarily a social phenomenon of the history." He goes on to say, "Within three centuries, however, the situation, and with it the character of assembly changed radically. In sharp contrast to the catch-as-catch-can house churches depicted in Acts, stands the monumental church building. One is seemingly random and informal; the other is hieratic and fixed. From the fourth century onward, the basilica (the epitome of Christian church architecture) became a norm of style."

In this early stage of the development of the church, it is interesting to note that Christians weren't the only groups that met in homes. Jews scattered by the Diaspora met in homes before they could erect temples. Also, academic discussion groups called *collegia* were home-based. At this point none of these small sect-like groups experienced persecution or disfavor. In fact, in some ways the commoners in the community respected these groups because the hosts were often wealthy and prestigious. At this stage, early Christians weren't viewed differently from other groups in the community. According to White, "In buying houses, maintaining extended household relations, or adapting houses for communal assembly, Christians were fully in touch with the world around them. Christians lived and operated within the bounds of society at large."

Eventually the venue for meeting would change for all groups. According to White, these early Christians would begin to use larger buildings to accommodate their growing congregations. It was around A.D. 250 that the first worship centers for Christians emerged. Buildings that were initially used for small house church groups were expanded into dedicated worship centers. Wall murals indicate religious themes that were specific to congregational usage. By the fourth century, worship centers had become more elaborate. They began to appear throughout the Middle East and the Mediterranean.

As a part of the Radical Reformation in the 1500s, our ancestors abandoned their connections with the cathedrals of Europe. Given the fact that they were rebelling against what they considered to be the excesses of the Catholics and the Protestants, it isn't surprising that they chose simple places to worship. They hid out in caves, barns, and in homes for safety. But this choice was also based on their understanding of the Bible. The early Anabaptists were scattered throughout the countryside and into the mountains and had no centralized organization to assist them. They wanted nothing to do with the kind of Christianity that boasted of its cathedrals while sending Anabaptists to death. It is understandable that Anabaptists have rejected elaborate buildings ever since.

Some of our ancestors who left Europe landed in Germantown, Pennsylvania, in 1683. They didn't erect a permanent building for worship until 1708. A simple limestone building replaced the original meeting house and stands at the same site in what is now northwest Philadelphia. Although thousands of Mennonite church buildings were erected around the world since that time, most would be small and simple in form. None would be temples or cathedrals. The median Mennonite congregation has 72 members, too small to need a large building.

The charter members at AMC decided to build our present church on a 13 ½ -acre field on the southeast edge of the village of Akron. Of all things, tobacco was being grown at this site! In fact, the church is located a block from Tobacco Road and five blocks from where cigars had been manufactured. God told Moses on Mount Horeb to remove his sandals because "the place upon which you are standing is holy ground." By contrast, our founders must have wondered if a tobacco field could ever become holy ground for our people. Surely they envisioned something more life giving than tobacco to come from this soil.

From our *high place*—Akron—we overlook the fertile Conestoga Valley. As far as we can see, Mennonites and Amish farmers work the lush fields in what is often called the *Garden Spot* of Pennsylvania. It has become our promised land. It is literally a land flowing with milk and honey.

In 1959, Akron was a village of 2,167 citizens. Its main industries were shoe manufacturing and tobacco processing. Many adults worked in nearby Ephrata or in Lancaster City. At that time, Lancaster County had 278,359 residents and was just beginning to awaken as a major metropolitan area. Today Akron has 4,018 residents and the population of Lancaster County has burgeoned to over a half million people. This area has become a part of the East Coast megalopolis. When flying over the region it is hard to see many large open tracts of land left between the county and Philadelphia.

During the discernment process for our original building project, AMC members engaged Mennonite attorney Samuel S. Wenger

Groundbreaking: Ura Gingerich with shovel, September 16, 1962.

to assist them in their decision-making. As one of the
first attorneys in the Mennonite church, Wenger
was in many respects a
forward-looking person.
He gave an enthusiastic
push for AMC to become
a flagship church for more
progressive and cosmopoli-
tan Mennonites. He envi-

Model of proposed church (never completed as proposed), 1962.

sioned that our building would be large enough to host regional meetings. His son Sam and daughter-in-law Ruth have been members at
AMC since 1966.

To move forward with building plans, a committee asked architect Weldon Bender to draw up plans *that reflected our faith*. That
request included building a Sunday School wing along with a fellowship hall that could double as a worship center. The planners were es-

pecially concerned that adequate space be provided for Christian education and fellowship needs. The building was obviously kept simple and understated as a statement of their lifestyle.

Bender presented a two-stage design that, in its second stage, would create an auditorium to seat up to 650 people! That size was what attorney Wenger was hoping for. Although some members were frightened at the size of the project, they decided to move forward with the first stage. Indeed, by 1960 they had already raised the $13,500 to pay for 13 ½ acres in Akron by having each family contribute one week's wages. When the first shovel was turned for the new building, in 1962, they had raised $60,000, leaving a total of $45,000 of borrowed money that was paid off in 8 ½ years.

The original design called for an education wing positioned perpendicular to nearby Diamond Street and joined at the rear by a fellowship hall. That hall would double as the sanctuary for the next 26 years. With folding chairs, the room seated about 250 people. The building might have appeared to be a school or an office building from the street. A main entrance was not obvious. The visual point of reference was the blunt end of the education wing. There wasn't even a hint of cathedralism!

On the day of the groundbreaking ceremony, September 16, 1962, a picture shows 13 men dressed in dark suits and narrow ties (one in a bow tie), two women and one boy. They were standing stiffly watching Ura Gingerich drive the symbolic shovel into the shale soil where the tobacco once grew. Slightly to Ura's left, matron Edna Byler stands Bible in hand, giving a maternal blessing to the occasion. The building was finished in 1963. The process was slowed down briefly when *water witches* were unable to discover enough water on site to supply the building. After drilling two weak wells, the leaders were able to convince the Borough of Akron to hook the church onto a water main.

Because of a rapidly expanding membership and an increasing number of children, this new facility became stretched to capacity

AMC, front of Sunday School wing, November 1969.

Interior of original AMC sanctuary (the current fellowship hall), 1977.

in just a few years. By the late 1960s, the membership had already doubled. The fire chief of Akron expressed concern that the building was occupied beyond capacity, especially in the fellowship hall during worship. The chairs had been placed closer to each other to accommodate the growing congregation, and the aisles were still uncomfortably narrow. Usher John Hostetler notes that it was becoming difficult to escort people to their seats. Member Sam Wenger remembers drawing up a new seating arrangement to make the fellowship hall safer.

Temporary space for an office and a classroom was secured by purchasing a nearby house. Several years later two classroom trailers were also purchased. For a brief time, the church experimented with having two services but that proved unsatisfactory and was discontinued. Few people attended the second service and there was some concern that having two services would split the congregation.

Recognizing that more space was needed, the congregation studied various options for six years before they overwhelmingly approved a revised expansion plan. It is clear that the group didn't want to use the original architect's plan to build a large sanctuary. That step was too big for them. They were resisting the idea of becoming a large congregation. The congregation's answer was to gain more seating space by rotating the layout in the fellowship hall by a quarter turn. At what would then become the back of the room, a new adjacent foyer with sliding glass doors made room for people who couldn't fit in the main hall. However, that design created its own problems on mornings when the overflow crowd spilled over into the foyer. It was hard for these people to feel that they were a part of the congregation.

The renovation was completed in 1977 at a cost of $150,000. The church borrowed $42,900 to cover the remainder of the costs. Membership at that point was 256. The addition also created an office for the pastor, a nursery, a library, and several restrooms. A basement under the new wing provided additional classrooms for adults, an MYF room, and a place for storage.

AMC Nursery, from left to right: Dylan Nolt, Bree Beyer, Cyndy Zook, and Mara Zimmerman, 2009.

Within two years, the children ran out of space for Sunday School and were given part of the adult space. Some of the adults had to leave the grounds for classes in nearby homes and at MCC facilities several blocks away. By 1984 it had become evident that the building would need to be expanded again, especially the worship space.

After much debate, architect Robert Beers was asked to draw up a design for a larger building. His drawings, approved by a 79.5 percent vote, included a 500-seat sanctuary, more office space, three classrooms for adults, and a new and larger MYF room. Four classrooms for children were added to the education wing, plus space for an office and storage for the Diamond Street Preschool Center was created.

There was considerable discussion about whether the new sanctuary should have benches or stacking chairs. Some members wanted to avoid benches because permanent seating would make the sanctuary less flexible for other uses. Perhaps reflecting the changing demographics of the congregation, benches were chosen, although not without

Architect's presentation, addition to Sunday School wing, new sanctuary and offices: Paul Longacre, Rollin Rheinheimer, and architect, 1985.

Groundbreaking for sanctuary/office addition: Urbane Peachey, Naomi Wyble, Randy Shank (Puljek-Shank), Rollin Rheinheimer, Herman Bontrager, Clayton Martin, Dean Good, and architects, 1987.

controversy. Some older members welcomed the comfort of padded benches and believed that benches would add to the aesthetics of the sanctuary. The members who wanted chairs were concerned about the costs incurred by having benches. They also felt that benches suggested too much traditionalism. In the end, the bench constituency won, although not without some bruised feelings. Some of those bruises are still detectable. The cost for this expansion was just over one million dollars. When construction began in 1987 our membership was 340.

Near the end of the building project, the contractors averted a tragedy when the roof of the sanctuary began sagging as the temporary support poles were being removed. Only the quick response of the workers prevented a collapse. The beams were re-engineered and we have gathered safely under this roof ever since. This glitch, however, slowed down the completion by about a year. On a cold February morning in 1989 we assembled in the old fellowship hall and with songbooks in hand walked to the new sanctuary for our first service in that room. Dedication services were held on April 2, 1989.

In reflecting on our struggle over the years to provide adequate space for our programs at AMC, pastor Urbane Peachey said in a newspaper interview on May 22, 1987, "Our space has always been behind our demand. We've always given priority to contributing our money to *people* causes rather than to building, and we've tried to emphasize giving for needs for other parts of the country and the world. We have, in all these years, cramped ourselves in terms of needed space."

For a period of time after the most recent expansion, we continued to grow. In the minutes of Church Council of May 1997, it was noted, "The sanctuary has been filled to the point that chairs were added to the back, mostly during Advent, Easter, and funerals. Sunday mornings are becoming very full so that there is very little room for growth." In addressing the need, Congregational Chair Jim Smucker said, "Long-range planning of the building and property is a long-range goal that will be addressed in the next year." He appointed a task force to deal with growth. However, two years later they concluded that, "AMC's

Choir rehearsal before first service in new sanctuary, February 5, 1989.

New sanctuary, February 5, 1989.

present facilities should not be expanded. It fits the needs of Diamond Street Early Childhood Center and AMC within existing walls." There was some feeling that we could find better ways to use our existing space. There were no further details provided.

A vision retreat in 2002 looked again at the overall needs of the congregation. The participants discussed the need to find ways to renew our worship and community life, and to engage in new mission. They also suggested that we examine our organizational structure.

Because of our continued growth in attendance, space issues once again surfaced at the retreat. A study committee was created to examine this issue. After a time of review they recommended adding to the building. They highlighted the need for a larger fellowship hall and more classroom space for adults. No mention was made of needing more room in the sanctuary.

A decision was made to hire architect Dale Yoder to present a long-term plan for dealing with our need for more space. His fifteen-year multi-phase plan included large-scale changes, including rerouting the main driveway, building a large multi-purpose facility that would serve as a recreation center and dining hall, and adding another office. He also suggested improvements that would meet the needs of the DSECC. The most important part of the plan was to create a new kitchen and dining room. His long-range plan also projected a 900-seat amphitheater-type sanctuary.

Because the plan seemed too expansive for the congregation, the committee scaled it down. They recommended building a fellowship hall and a new kitchen. They also proposed converting the present fellowship hall into adult Sunday School classrooms. Their revised plan, however, was defeated in March 2006 when it failed by a few votes to receive the required two-thirds majority.

There was passion on both sides of this issue. Those in favor of the building plan felt that the new facilities were vital to the church. Those opposed reflected the congregational ethos of simplicity and also sensitivity to the needs of churches in developing countries.

There was also some concern about the potential lack of financial support.

In spite of all of the additions to our facilities over the years, the building is still inadequate in very significant ways. The Fellowship Hall remains too small to seat the entire congregation. That tends to limit the number of people who stay for meals. Also, there are not enough adequate spaces for Discipleship Hour classes. The spaces that are available tend to have noise intrusions or are rooms that do not facilitate personal sharing. With the presence of blackboards they suggest a school classroom.

Storage space continues to be an ongoing need. A committee recommended adding storage space onto the fellowship room in December 2006. That plan failed due to lack of support. Some people felt the proposal avoided addressing the overall need for more adequate facilities.

In a way it has been easier to take care of our dead than our living. We established a cemetery on 1.4 acres in 1978 without controversy. It provides 638 full-sized lots and 178 half-sized lots featuring flat pavers on the gravesites instead of standing memorial stones. Perhaps because we were aging as a congregation, it was important for us to have a permanent resting place for the deceased. That seemed more urgent than our temporal needs for church space for living members.

AMC Cemetery, 2009.

We had considered using 5.4 acres on our grounds for housing AMC seniors. However, that was defeated in 1994. Some of our land has been developed into a very attractive playground for both our children and for the children of DSECC. Recently the ground cover was changed to a rubber format for safety reasons and to meet the requirements of the state. In the meantime, the rest of our land is rented out to a local farmer.

God's people have always needed a place to gather. Most often that has required a building. Sometimes those buildings are simple, sometimes elaborate, but most often moderate. It is hard for a church to exist without a roof, a wall and a floor. Although Mennonites don't depend on steeples or stained glass windows to define our meetinghouses, we still need space to worship, to study together, to eat, and for other activities.

One of the most difficult decisions a congregation makes is whether to build or to remodel. It may be especially so in Mennonite churches where every member has a vote. Being congregational in polity, without priests, hierarchy, or denominational ownership, members often struggle with this decision. At AMC we have spent many hours deliberating about our building. Because of our international sensitivities, we feel uncomfortable when we spend money on ourselves.

Being pilgrims on our way to somewhere else, we sometimes avoid looking at present as well as future needs. And with many of us being more concerned with the process than the product, we sometimes labor needlessly to make up our mind. Discussion trumps decision. We have made attempts to deal with this issue over the years. Presently, even though our average attendance is down, we still need additional space to carry out the mission of AMC. It is an issue that we must face if we are to grow numerically, spiritually, and affectionately.

Chapter Six

Pilgrims' Gifts

"THE GIFTS HE GAVE WERE THAT SOME WOULD BE APOSTLES, SOME PROPHETS, SOME EVANGELISTS, SOME PASTORS AND TEACHERS, TO EQUIP THE SAINTS FOR THE WORK OF MINIS-TRY, FOR BUILDING UP THE BODY OF CHRIST...."

EPHESIANS 4:11-12 (NRSV)

"HE LOOKED UP AND SAW RICH PEOPLE PUTTING THEIR GIFTS INTO THE TREASURY; HE ALSO SAW A POOR WIDOW PUT IN TWO SMALL COPPER COINS. HE SAID, "TRULY I TELL YOU, THIS POOR WIDOW HAS PUT IN MORE THAN ALL OF THEM; FOR ALL OF THEM HAVE CONTRIBUTED OUT OF THEIR ABUNDANCE, BUT SHE OUT OF HER POVERTY HAS PUT IN ALL SHE HAD TO LIVE ON."

LUKE 21:1-4 (NRSV)

Our gifts at AMC are expressed through giving our money and our talents. We have a long and rich history of doing both. We are unusually blessed with generous persons who reach into their pockets for their last coin as well as persons who give unselfishly from deeper pockets. We have also served as medical missionaries in poor countries as well as medical missionaries to the poor in our community. Recently we rebuilt the sagging porch of a neighbor of one of our members. Members showed up on a Saturday morning with tools in hand and restored the porch to its prime.

Other members go to far-off places to rebuild houses destroyed by hurricanes, like the one in Cameron, Louisiana, for the Conner family that our crews rebuilt in December 2008. Overcoming problems from an additional storm that washed out the new pillars, our crew returned to complete the project. Some of our members, including Project Director Bob Wyble and Construction Supervisor Elvin Stoltzfus, were at the site for nearly a month. Businessman Rick Haller and two of his managers installed the plumbing and wiring. Delores Nolt and her sister staffed a food stand to feed hungry workers during the busiest week of the project. It moved forward in spite of heavy rains. The workers learned how to deal with mud. It is unclear whether they or the grateful family received the greater blessings from the project.

Richard and Ruth Weaver were invited by MCC in 1994 to serve as trauma counselors in the refugee camps following the Rwandan genocide. They were encouraged in their mission by Myron Ebersole, chaplain at the Hershey Medical Center. Before they left for Africa he hand delivered to them two copies of Henri Nouwen's *Our Greatest*

AMC-MDS project in Louisiana: wall construction on AMC parking lot, 2008.

Conner family: Vicky and David Conner, Victoria and David, Jr., 2008.

AMC-MDS project in Louisiana, 2008.

Gift; a Meditation on Dying and Caring. This inspired book and the sensitivity of Chaplain Ebersole carried them through some difficult experiences.

Those of us who have stayed close to home use our gifts to serve as teachers, social workers, attorneys, businesspersons, sales people, office workers, homemakers, and in other capacities. AMC members have always been active in serving our community as volunteers. Indeed, a study of the congregation several years ago found that we give at least three times more volunteer time in the community than we do within the church. At least six of our members have belonged to the local Lions Club, which raises funds for eyeglasses and to make improvements in the Akron Park. In addition they constructed a fence for the *service dog* of a local blind woman. Giving is something we consider our privilege.

Giving is something we know is our responsibility.

Our views of giving have been deeply influenced by our relationship with MCC, various mission boards, and other church agencies such as Mennonite Economic Development Associates, Mennonite Disaster Service, and Ten Thousand Villages. Indeed, one of our own, the late Edna Byler, was instrumental in starting the Self Help Crafts program (later to be renamed Ten Thousand Villages). In the beginning she sold products made in Puerto Rico and the Middle East. She opened the first store in 1946 in her basement and occasionally took her products on the road, using the trunk of her car as her venue. Edna had a deep passion for these new and unique products from other countries and for the artisans who produced them.

Edna Byler: photo from Mennonite Central Committee, 1965.

Since then, Ten Thousand Villages has expanded to 36 countries and now has annual revenues of 39 million dollars from its 127 stores and other outlets. Several of its administrators, numerous staff, and volunteers have been members of AMC. A former administrator, Paul Myers, is now the director of the International Federation of Alternative Trade. Other AMC members have also gone outside the Mennonite community to serve with various interdenominational health and welfare agencies. Ron Hunsicker is the President and CEO of the National Association of Addiction Treatment Programs.

In the 1950s and 1960s, some AMCers served in overseas alternative service programs like Pax, while others spent time in voluntary service programs or in 1-W service in hospitals. In more recent years, some of our young members have spent time in other cultures to fulfill cross-cultural service requirements at Mennonite colleges.

In the first year of our existence as a congregation, we took an offering to support the MCC meat canner program and several years later we actually helped with the canning. Even though the term *missional* has become the term *de jour*, AMC has been on a mission from day one. The following is a partial list of some of the ways that is demonstrated:

LOCAL HOUSING

Pastor Kermit Derstine prodded members in 1967 to buy and refurbish a house in Lancaster city for a disadvantaged family. Later, in a similar way, a house was provided for a needy family in Ephrata. At about the same time, AMC member Art Voth played an important role in the founding of Menno Housing (now Tabor Community Services) in Lancaster. He was the first recording secretary for this organization that originally sought to make housing available for minority persons in Lancaster. At that point there was still a great deal of racial discrimination in housing. Tabor has become a multidimensional housing and financial counseling agency that serves as a model for the State of Pennsylvania and has received national acclaim.

We have had extensive involvement in the Habitat for Humanity program both nationally and locally. Edgar Stoesz was elected as the national board chair while other AMC members served on the local board. We have also volunteered at the Water Street Rescue Mission, a program for the homeless in Lan-

Art Voth, 1999.

caster County. In recent years we have supported the Homes of Hope program in Ephrata, an interdenominational effort to create low-cost housing for disadvantaged people in our community.

DISASTER RELIEF

As in the story of the crew from AMC who recently rebuilt a house in Louisiana, we have been very generous in responding to natural disasters both stateside and abroad. Much of this work has been done under the aegis of Mennonite Disaster Service. Indeed, it was a former AMCer, Peter Dyck, who helped expand the nascent Mennonite Service Organization into a church wide organization in 1952. What was only a regional, small effort by local Mennonites in Kansas would become the binational Mennonite Disaster Service in 1955. Most of its administrators have been members of AMC. Following overseas disasters, our members contribute money and goods though MCC. Reg Toews and Ron Mathies, former MCC administrators, were members at AMC. Numerous department leaders and other workers at MCC have been or continue to be members at AMC.

WAR-RELATED ASSISTANCE

Some of our members have lived in war zones during times of strife. Most were there as representatives of MCC doing relief and service missions. Peter and Elfrieda Dyck, who later became members at AMC, performed this kind of service in Europe during World War II. They were instrumental in the resettlement of refugees from Russia, Poland, and Germany through the boatlifts to Paraguay in the 1950s. That story is well told in their book *Up From The Rubble.* Two of our families, the Habeggers and the Neufelds, came from war-torn Europe with their parents at about the same time. However, they came under the sponsorship of Lancaster Mennonite families.

Refugee resettlement continues to be an important mission at AMC. Over the years we have resettled at least eight refugee families from

Peter and Elfrieda Dyck, 2001.

seven countries. Recently we welcomed the Jabri family from Iraq. They had also experienced the pain of war. Members of AMC have accompanied them throughout the process of adapting to the United States.

We were especially active in theatres of conflict during the Vietnam War. The Paul Leatherman family hid under stairways in Saigon during the 1968 Tet offensive. Lynne Sensenig Brubaker, who was five years old when her family was in Vietnam, has memories of seeing the lights of the gunfire from the roof of their house in Saigon and of feeling *cooped up* for one week while the battle raged on. She and her sister were able to wander away from their property through an open gate in their yard. Much to their mother's dismay—and relief—the girls ended up at a neighbor's house while the battle was going on. During this same time, other members of AMC were active in peacemaking in Vietnam and attempted to clarify to both sides that they were in Vietnam as examples of Christ's love, not as representatives of the American government.

While some of us were in the war zone, others at AMC took to the streets to protest the war. Several members withheld taxes as a symbolic protest. In more recent times, a number of us have become bumper-sticker peace advocates who announce the folly of war from our vehicles. This form of witness has become a kind of moving billboard stating— *God bless the whole world, no exceptions.* John Shearer and Al Claassen were responsible for borrowing and enlarging this slogan from MCC. They have now distributed approximately 3,600 copies. In more recent years, John Stoner played a significant

Bumper sticker, 2009.

role in founding Every Church a Peace Church and Michael and Lorri Hardin founded Preaching Peace.

Although AMCers are generally pacifists, some aren't comfortable with protesting the actions of the government. They would be inclined to only pray for peace and for our national leaders. This can be a point of tension at AMC, especially if the issues are attached to political parties. Mostly, this conflict is not expressed openly within the church, perhaps because the peace position is predominant in the church. People who have a different opinion refrain from speaking out because they don't want to create conflict.

INVOLVEMENT WITH THE INTERNATIONAL/NATIONAL MENNONITE CHURCH

We have been supportive of the Mennonite World Conference—a loosely connected federation of various Anabaptist denominations scattered around the world. Currently this body represents approximately 1.5 million members in 53 countries. An AMC associate member Nancy Heisey has served as the President of MWC. Our international connections have also been expressed through collegial relationships with churches in Argentina and Honduras. We have sent delegations to these countries and have hosted some of their leaders here.

Stateside we have had relationships with emerging churches within our Atlantic Coast Conference. For many years that relationship has been with Friendship Community Church in New York City. We have also been involved since 1969 with Camp Deerpark in upstate New York, a facility that serves the Mennonite churches in New York City. AMC members have served on their Board. Don Gunden was Board Chair for many years.

We were active in the process that led to the merger of the Mennonite Church and the General Conference Mennonite Church—now the *Mennonite Church USA.* AMC was a dual-conference church

ACC/Argentina Partnership: Daniel Galmer, Domingo and Teresa Figueiras, Patricio Figueiras with Eileen and Lester Graybill, 2003.

International Mission/Food Festival: Dave Frey and Menno Diener, 1997.   *International Missions Weekend/Food Festival: Anita Brendle, 1997.*

beginning in 1974, which motivated us to play a role in creating this new unified denomination. The merger became official in 2001. Former member, Vern Preheim, was a central figure in the merger and guided it during the period of transition.

Involvement in Human Services

Our church has always been involved in meeting human needs through social agencies and hospitals. For many years we have joined neighboring churches on the CROP walk to raise money for food being sent to disadvantaged nations. Fifty-two AMCers raised $8,105 in the most recent walk.

We have also been active in a local agency, the Ephrata Area Social Services, to assist with meeting the food and financial needs of the disadvantaged in our own community. AMC members have served on their board. Our church foyer is occasionally filled with bags of gro-

Grocery bags for mission project, 2001.

ceries to be sent to New York City or to other places. We also collect school supplies, blankets, Christmas bundles, and other goods that are distributed by MCC.

Members were involved in setting up a local branch of the Recovery of Hope program for troubled marriages. This intensive program is based at Philhaven, a local mental health facility. Numerous members have worked at Philhaven in various capacities including administrator Phil Hess.

Several members have worked in hospitals, including Penn State-Hershey Medical Center, Lancaster General Hospital, and Ephrata Community Hospital. Over the years significant numbers of physicians, nurses, and other medical workers have been members of AMC. Some members have served as chaplains at these hospitals and at Hospice. Myron Ebersole served as president of the National College of Chaplains.

Ruth Weaver was instrumental in the expansion of Bridge of Hope (BOH), a local/national program that provides mentoring and assistance to single mothers. Several of our members have been active in raising funds for this program and many more have given generously of their time and money. The primary fundraiser for BOH is a banquet in which nationally known speakers are the focal point of the event. Ruth Weaver and Glenn Weaver have served on the local and the national boards, Ruth as Chair. AMC is in the process of becoming a mentoring congregation for a BOH family.

Ruth and Lowell Detweiler were the founders of No Longer Alone Ministries, a regional program to meet the needs of families with relatives who have a chronic mental illness. Other AMC members have served with Contact, a crisis phone line for people experiencing emotional turmoil.

Ruth and Lowell Detweiler, 2001.

Our church has been involved as volunteers in prison ministries over the years. John and Kathy Hostetler made monthly visits for sixteen years to the Federal Correctional Institution-Schuylkill, a prison that is 55 miles from Akron. Former member Howard Zehr was the founder of the Victim-Offender Reconciliation Program that now has both national and local expressions. He was instrumental in developing the concept of bringing victims and their offenders together to create forgiveness. He has been called the *grandfather of the restorative justice concept.* He is currently a professor in the Restorative Justice and Peacebuilding program at Eastern Mennonite University in Harrisonburg, Virginia.

DIAMOND STREET EARLY CHILDHOOD CENTER

This signature program of AMC was started in 1969 as a nursery school for the Akron/Ephrata community. One year later Headstart, a local Community Action Program for disadvantaged children, rented two classrooms in our education wing. They operated in our building as a parallel program with separate staffing and funding until 1992.

The nursery school expanded over the years. In 1985 daycare was added to the program, necessitating a name change to Diamond Street Preschool Center (DSPC). When the Headstart program left our building, classroom space was opened up, making it possible to add after-school and summer daycare programs. DSPC then became the Diamond Street Early Childhood Center (DSECC) and now serves an average of 125 students. For legal reasons DSECC transferred their ownership in 1999 to a local social service agency as a conduit for the provision of medical and retirement benefits for its employees.

As a mission of AMC, DSECC attempts to be a welcoming place for families with young children. Although parents are grateful for this high quality program, only two families have chosen to make AMC their church home. Numerous members of AMC have volunteered at DSECC; several have served on the board and some of the directors and staff members

DSECC: Sheryl Krafft with DSECC student, 2008.

have also come from our congregation. Some of our members have laundered the mats that the children use for their naptime.

In 2008 the program was awarded the highest level for excellence: Four Stars in the Keystone STARS program—a statewide body that measures quality in day care programs. In addition, DSECC has also been accepted as the first day care program in the Mennonite Education Agency. The MEA is made up of Mennonite schools from

DSECC: Celebration of STAR designation: June Hershberger and Kathy Stephens, 2008.

kindergarten through college, graduate school and seminary. DSECC attempts to provide safe, loving care in a peace-oriented environment as an expression of the larger Mennonite ethos. Through scholarships, fundraisers, and in-kind gifts, AMC subsidizes the DSECC budget by about $30,000 annually.

The double use of the building and grounds by DSECC and the Christian Education Department at AMC is an ongoing challenge. The presence of materials that are required for DSECC's program can compete for space with the Sunday School and other needs of AMC. The problem has become more significant as DSECC has expanded. There are no easy answers to this ongoing issue.

College Scholarship Fund

In 1978, AMC made a commitment to provide financial assistance to our college students attending Mennonite/Anabaptist Colleges. The original charter of the scholarship program made a grant available to a minority student not from AMC. Lennardo Torres from Brooklyn was the first minority recipient in 1981. In the same year Elke Goertz from Waynseboro was granted a scholarship based on financial need. Both of these students were connected with Atlantic Coast Conference churches. The record of the scholarship fund committee does not reveal anything about the outcome of their education. It is known that they applied for help for only one year. Perhaps more minority scholarships were not given out, in part, because it was hard for the committee to connect with minorities who wanted to attend one of the Mennonite institutions.

For a brief period scholarships were given to AMC students attending Messiah College. That was discontinued when the college diminished its affiliation with the founding denomination, the Brethren in Christ Church.

While some parents of students attending non-Mennonite schools felt the scholarship program should not be tied to a Mennonite institution, the congregation voted to stay with the original charter. This decision was based for the most part on loyalty to church institutions. It was also believed that the church schools could have a more positive influence on the students' long-term bonding with the Mennonite church. Another part of the rationale was that our tax dollars were already subsidizing the state system and that many grants and loans were available to students who attended non-Mennonite institutions.

In the first year of the program, each student was given a scholarship of $500. That amount has now increased to $3,000. The peak year for the number of scholarships was 1999 when 22 students received support. In the most recent year, 14 students received assistance. The fund got its impetus from several members who set up endowment funds in the early 1970s to support students who chose Mennonite Higher Education. Now most of the funds are raised through the annual pig roast and auction. In each of the last four years, $20,000 to $25,000 has been raised. Over the 30 years of its existence, approximately a half million dollars has been given to AMC students attending Mennonite institutions.

NEEDS WITHIN THE CONGREGATION

A Brotherhood Fund (now Agape Fund) was begun in 1961 to meet the unexpected financial needs of AMCers. Sixty-four dollars was distributed in the first year; $4,100 was given out in 2008. The fund is primarily managed by the pastoral team and operates with confidentiality and sensitivity. Gifts can be given to cover medical expenses, rent assistance, or for other needs.

The Committee on Congregational Life sends flowers and works closely with house churches and other groups to provide meals when a member is in a crisis. Transportation can also be provided for medical appointments or for other practical needs. The Hospitality Committee provides meals for funerals and other events. In 2007 the congregation voted to establish a part-time Special Care Minister position to reach out to members with parapastoral needs, especially those members over 65.

Over the years, house church groups have played a vital role in meeting the needs of members within AMC. An example of that can be is seen in the house church response to the needs of Phil and Marian Rutt and their son Phillip, who developed cerebral palsy at birth. Their house church group has stood by them in various ways, including arranging for Phillip's care while Phil and Marian took their adopted daughter Elizabeth to visit her ancestral home in Vietnam. Longtime friends Jim and Donna Shenk, who coordinated the care, also arrange for Phillip's care during Discipleship Hour and on evenings when the Rutts need some respite.

The Rutts also formed a special friendship with Lloyd and Nancy Chapman, a couple they met while their children were clients at the Susquehanna Association for the Blind. Through that friendship, the Chapmans became members at AMC and are a vital part of the Rutt's house church group.

The Pilgrims' Money

AMC has been generous in giving from its material resources. On our first Sunday 50 years ago, we collected $130 in the offering. Now we give on average, $12,288 each Sunday to meet our current budget of $639,000. Our giving has always supported needs both within the congregation and beyond. Throughout our history we have consistently met our budgets, albeit with heavy December giving. We have gone far beyond the budget to pay for new buildings and for other projects. In addition, our members individually support many causes that are outside the congregation and are unreported in any of the accountability streams. Some estimates suggest that we give twice as much to causes that are off the budget.

Since the church-wide merger forming the MC USA, we no longer have to divide our resources between the two original denominations. That has made budgeting easier. Although it isn't clear whether we individually tithe at the ten percent level, what is known is that we are very generous in sharing our money.

There is concern that some slippage in stewardship has occurred in recent years. It is unclear whether that is happening primarily with younger members who might have a different view of stewardship. What is known is that many of our members are now retired and on fixed incomes. Whatever the case, budgeting has become tighter. In 2008 a task force was appointed to examine church finances, especially as they relate to demographics, attendance, staffing costs, and other factors. This is an unsettled issue.

We have always been generous pilgrims. Generous with the ways we reach out to our many communities through acts of service. Generous with the ways we give our money to support the congregation and the broader world. We have been unusually blessed with the talents of members who lead, create, administer, and serve. When the time comes to reach for the coin, we also respond generously. When we are given a call to build up the body of Christ, we hear that plea as well. Our journey has taken us to places of need at home and abroad. The journey continues.

"... what is known is that we are very generous in sharing our money," 1975.

Chapter Seven

The Spiritual Journey

Early in our history, the spiritual identity of AMC was described as *cutting edge*. For many years we were noticeably different from our Mennonite neighbors. In some ways we were even a step ahead of the broader Mennonite church in both our theology and practice.

Perhaps we got this identity because many of us came to AMC with international experiences and advanced education. Maybe it came from having members who were leaders in the community as professionals and businesspersons. Whatever the cause, our differences were obvious to people in the nearby Mennonite community. One charter member says we might have acquired this reputation because there was *a streak of the rebel in us*.

If we have displayed hubris, it might be seen, for example, in the ways we value questions more than answers. We are more comfortable with ambiguity than we are with certainty. We can feel more passion about what we are *against* than what we are *for*. We are remarkably open to new ideas and to diversity, except when the ideas differ from ours. Authority can be regarded with suspicion and discomfort. Figuratively speaking, some of us still seem to be *quarreling with the Bishop*. Some of us have bad memories of strict rules about clothing, entertainment, and other forms of what were considered to be *worldliness*. After many years, some of us still feel both fear and anger toward authority figures.

On the other hand, AMC continues to be a prototype for Anabaptism. That means living, to some degree, in tension with the materialism and militarism in the surrounding secular culture. At the same time, we reject the forms of civil religion and prosperity gospel that dominate many conservative Protestant churches. The themes of peace and justice, servanthood, simple living, and discipleship have been a vital part of our spirituality throughout our fifty years.

We tend to be more comfortable talking about our personal relationship with God privately, however. There are some exceptions. Prior to emergency surgery to save her life, Esther Miller found herself praying, "Precious Lord, take my hand and never let it go." She repeated the phrase silently many times. As she was being wheeled into the operating room, she became aware of a nurse holding her hand and telling her, "Esther, I am here to be with you and to hold your hand. I will not let it go." Esther told that story with great relish and with great faith. She was convinced that the convergence of her prayers and the words of the nurse were more than a mere coincidence. We have a rich history of knowing God intimately and personally. We just don't talk about it publicly very much.

In our most recent vision statement we say: *AMC will be fully engaged in God's mission in a broken world as we are called, equipped and sent by the Holy Spirit to follow Christ in life. Shaped by the gifts and vision of our members, we will keep Christ and church at the center of our lives as we reach out to neighbors near and far, and witness to the world around us through an Anabaptist-Mennonite perspective.*

For the most part, we have lived up to this statement. Even though formal understandings like these aren't intended to be action plans, we do attempt to practice what we espouse in our written words. We give generously from our resources to various church programs. We attempt to be Christ-like examples in the workplace. We are remarkably involved as volunteers at many important and needy places. We bear witness to peace and justice themes in the various print media, join various witness marches, and resist paying *war taxes*. We are true to our vision statement by being peaceful citizens.

We recall with some nostalgia a high point in our spiritual life when one of our members, Doris Longacre, wrote the *More-With-Less Cookbook* in 1976. For this book, she involved many women at Akron and throughout the country in testing out recipes that people had submitted at her invitation. It was not the typical cookbook, however, because it was based on foods that were high in nutrition and high

in environmental sensitivity. It was her view that we needed to be stewards of our bodies and God's resources. She stressed simplicity and moderation in food consumption. The book made the *New York Times* bestseller book lists. She donated all of the proceeds from this book to MCC. In addition, her second book *Living More With Less*, published posthumously in 1979, had a profound impact on many of us at AMC.

Doris was unassuming in personality and not

Doris Longacre, 1976.

one to draw attention to herself. She was a tall Kansan, slightly bent in posture, who could appear tentative in her interactions. However, she was passionate about what she believed. She and her husband Paul shopped carefully and avoided chain stores and malls. Their theme was, "If it can't be bought on Main Street in Ephrata it doesn't need to be bought." She was especially opposed to war toys. On one occasion, she was effective in expressing her concerns to her congressman about the Vietnam War. As a former worker in Vietnam, she brought an Anabaptist perspective to him. Doris was the first woman Chairperson at AMC. She led the congregation well and helped to set a tone of tranquility and global awareness.

She had some influence in helping the congregation to scale down fellowship meals and her plea for simplicity was reflected in the building plans for our church. She also helped us keep our homes modest and our lifestyle contained. She died from cancer when she was thirty-nine.

But her cautionary spirit would slowly become muted. The next several decades brought unprecedented economic growth in our country. We, alongside of our neighbors, began to expand our consumerism. Climbing the economic and professional ladder was contagious. Our houses became larger, our cars more expensive, and our vacations more expansive. Instead of *living more with less* we began to *live more with more.* In many ways we were assimilating into the dominant culture. Simple living had become less important to us.

Gradually we began to work longer hours and many of us became two-income families. The free time activity level for families began to increase. It has become more common for us to seek respite at home or in recreational activities on Sunday morning. It is now more challenging to place the church at the center of our lives as we promised in our vision statement. Our attendance at worship is diminishing and our support of the various programs of the congregation is spottier. We are becoming more like the broader culture around us. This decline in allegiance to our mission statement took place over many years but has perhaps picked up speed in the last decade.

In the midst of all of this shaping and reshaping of our spirituality the mission of the church continues to move forward. The following narrative attempts to describe the ways the various programs illustrate the spiritual life at AMC.

WORSHIP

The style of the Sunday worship service has changed slightly over the years. In the beginning our worship style was less scripted, perhaps because the group was smaller. If the worship service was more spontaneous, we were, however, more formal in the ways we dressed. All the men wore ties and suits, and women were dressed in their Sunday best. We were more *buttoned down* then than we are today. Although the worship service included no liturgy, there was still a predictable routine. Piety and proper manners still ruled. We sat more stiffly and tried our best to make our children behave. The bulletins contained only announcements and a brief listing of the order of the morning service, usually including the sermon title.

In the last twenty-five years, our worship service has gradually become more formal through the increased use of litanies and rituals. Sermons are at times based on the lectionary and are the centerpiece of the morning service. A great deal of effort is put into connecting the sermon theme with the music and the other planned parts of the service. In contrast with the structured nature of the worship service, today the worshipers themselves appear less formal. More come dressed in sweaters and slacks. Some even come in blue jeans. We appear more relaxed in our demeanor and appear to worry less about the activities of our children during worship.

The more scripted style of the service has limited the amount of spontaneous personal sharing. We have a *roving mike* but that is used only to introduce visitors. Those introductions and announcements are now made at the beginning of the service. It is interesting to note that announcements have been a meaningful part of the worship experience. Who can forget the announcements that Peter Dyck made that morphed into homilies? Or how deeply Kevin King's tears touched us when he talked about the suffering he witnessed on one of his overseas assignments with MCC. And the MYF never fails to amuse us by their creative and unconventional announcements. In our present format, this brief moment of spontaneity ends when the worship leader—often accompanied by musicians—directs the congregation in a moment of quiet reflection as a transition to worship.

At the conclusion of the worship service, the pastor offers the benediction and then mingles with the congregation. Early in Kermit Derstine's term, he eliminated the pastoral-greeting-at-the-door ritual. He felt that members should greet each other. It was also an attempt to de-emphasize the elevated role of the pastor. Perhaps that set the tone for all the pastors who would follow. Recently the Church

Children's Story: Dawn Yoder Harms, 1997.

Council requested the pastors to occasionally be present at the doors to strengthen their connection with the worshippers.

There are several events during the year that often generate extra emotion and more informality during worship. These include the dedication of babies, baptisms, and the reception of new members. The children's story offered by one of the pastors each Sunday often adds spontaneity and energy. Not surprisingly, Christmas and Easter services are always highlights for the congregation.

MUSIC

Music has been an integral part of the worship experience over these fifty years. Indeed, we have held onto some very important musical traditions at AMC. We have been committed to simple, unaccompanied congregational singing. Because the congregation has many singers who are skillful in four-part harmony, the quality of singing has been high. Some persons believe the singing sounded better when we were in the previous sanctuary. It was smaller and the acoustics were much better. Now when attendance is down and the group is scattered in the sanctuary, the singing can be less vibrant.

However, the essence of four-part, unaccompanied singing remains central to our worship. Some songs are favorites of the congregation and create emotions that sweep over the worshippers, bringing joy or tears. At those moments it would seem that the Holy Spirit is especially palpable. Sometimes when we have guest speakers or on other special occasions, we celebrate by singing *606*—later to be assigned the number *118*—in the new *Worship Book*. We always sing the song with a spirit of joyfulness and sometimes to reassure ourselves that we are still *above average* in our singing!

In the early years, one of the members gave a significant gift to buy an organ. However, we didn't move ahead with the purchase because it was believed that an organ would interfere with congregational singing. In 1979 the donor's money was used instead to purchase a piano. Today the piano, drums, Orff instruments, guitars and other in-

Palm Sunday: Orff instruments played by Corin Kidwell, Emily Hartzler and Lindsay Garber, 1998.

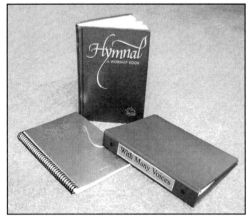

AMC hymnbooks, 2009.

struments are played during worship. Instruments occasionally accompany congregational singing, but that happens only when a particular song requires it.

Presently we sing from three songbooks, *The Worship Book, Sing and Rejoice* and a compilation of songs that we call *With Many Voices*. These books replaced several songbooks that were used sequentially over the years. Not only did the previous books show their age, some of the songs became anachronistic and by today's standard *politically incorrect*. To-

AMC Choir; Row 1: Kathy Good, Grace Brubaker, Anne Weaver, Joyce Haller, Sue Brubaker. Row 2: Jay Brubaker, Becky Good, Martha Hess, Zem Martin, Fritzi Nussbaum. Row 3: Merle Gingerich, Paul Burkholder, Sam Wenger, Rich Crockett, Daryl Garber, Jim Landis and Ken Langeman, 1986.

Men's Choir at ACC Vision Dinner; Warren Leatherman, leader. Back row: Bruce McCrae, H.A. Penner, Don Good, Eric Habegger, Seth Ebersole, Rollin Rheinheimer, Marvin Nolt, David Moyer. Front row: Daryl Eshleman, Merle Gingerich, Don Mellinger, Menno Diener, Richard Weber, Rich Crockett, and Brian Weaver, September 26, 2000.

day we use many new and transcultural songs that bring color to the worship experience. We have assiduously avoided forming a worship team as is now common in many other Christian churches. Instead of being led by performers on stage, we prefer to have a single song leader who conducts the congregation from the stage. That pattern has not changed over our 50 years together. However, there is some concern about needing to re-examine our worship style.

Our first adult choir was formed in 1959 and has been an important part of our worship services over the years. The choir now sings occasionally during worship and for special events. More recently, the participation of members decreased to the point that the viability of a mixed choir was in doubt. A switch in rehearsal time from Wednesday night to early Sunday morning brought choir members back with new enthusiasm.

We also have had a vigorous men's choir as a part of worship since their beginning in 1990. They usually sing monthly. This choir often sings some of the older and more traditional hymns. These hymns have a unique way of connecting emotionally with the people in the pews. Occasionally, the men's choir, too, struggles to find enough members.

Children's choir, 1976.

Preschool choir: Karen King and Linda Frey, Christmas 1995.

Children's music has always been a vital part of worship at AMC. Indeed, at one point there were three separate children's choirs. Now with fewer children in the congregation, they sing less often. Men's quartets, women's trios, and other groups have been a valuable part of our history, especially in earlier years. An orchestra,

25th AMC Anniversary Celebration trio: Anne Weaver, Grace Brubaker, and Helen Peifer, 1984.

made up of adults and children, also performs on occasion. On almost every Sunday instrumentalists play preludes and offertories. Sometimes we have a hymn sing during the pre-service time.

COMMUNION

In the beginning years at AMC, communion was served two times a year. Initially, Gladys Stoesz baked the bread in what she describes as *little marble sized pieces*. As the church grew, a number of women began baking traditional loaves of bread for communion. John and Janet Weber supplied the grape juice from their vineyard for about 15 years. Now both the bread and the grape juice are bought at a neighborhood grocery store.

Communion has been served quarterly in the recent years. That change took place during the term of Pastor Peachey. He developed a new appreciation for the place of communion in worship when he and his family attended services in the Greek Orthodox Church while they were living in Jordan. The increase in frequency was widely accepted and gave the Eucharist new importance to the people at AMC. It was his belief that communion should be experienced as an expression of God's grace, not as God's condemnation. He also advocated for the introduction of healing services, including the sacrament of anointing with oil.

Over the years pastors and lay leaders have distributed the elements in a variety of ways. Most recently, they have begun to use the *intinction* method of dipping the bread in the grape juice before the

Communion, 2009.

congregation consumes the elements. Communion is open to persons who are baptized Christians. From time to time there has been controversy about whether children should be permitted to participate. The congregation has consistently discouraged that idea although some parents have been disappointed with that decision.

The fall communion is celebrated on Worldwide Communion Sunday. It is interesting to note that in spite of our earlier controversy about women's head coverings, some of the women who now serve communion do indeed wear head coverings on this Sunday. However, the covering is one that is typical for the country being represented.

We practice foot washing following the Maundy Thursday service. While many of us grew up with foot washing as a part of our communion experience, some of us didn't and are uncomfortable with this practice, perhaps for reasons of privacy and modesty. In a similar way, the greeting of each other with a holy kiss after the foot washing has been a difficult ritual to retain. Only part of the congregation chooses to participate in the Maundy Thursday service. In a recent study by Conrad Kanagy, it was noted that foot washing is in decline throughout the Mennonite church.

Arts and Symbols

The Arts and Symbols Committee was formed in 1989 to incorporate spiritual symbols at various places within the church. That is somewhat in contrast with the Mennonite tradition of seeing a church building only as *a meetinghouse* unadorned with icons, stained glass windows, and elaborate symbols. Indeed the architecture and décor of AMC has been simple and utilitarian.

Members with an artistic bent now introduce us to various forms of art that enrich the worship experience. Among their projects was the establishment of a communion table replete with the Christ Candle and other symbols. The artists have also created various wall hangings, seasonal displays, and an arts table at the main entrance to the sanctuary.

Lenten display: Earthen vessels, 2000.

Epiphany candles, 1999.

CHRISTIAN EDUCATION

From early on, the congregation felt strongly that Christian education for adults and children was central to the spiritual life of the church. The name for the adult program has changed from *Sunday School* to *Christian Education,* and now to *Discipleship Hour*. The purpose has essentially remained the same, although the changes in name reflect subtle shifts in emphasis.

In the beginning we followed the International Sunday School series. Soon the curriculum was expanded to include an elective system that offered book studies and contemporary topics. Most of the classes were intergenerational. Clearly, we attempted to leave behind the rather restraining system of Sunday School that many of us had experienced growing up. This new approach, renamed Christian Education, was group-centered rather than teacher-centered. The Christian Education Committee selected the topics and the leaders. The classes would run for three months.

Christian Education class: Don Mellinger, Kathleen Roth, Alfred Claassen, Peter Passage, and Sue Passage, 1997.

This approach worked well for many years, but gradually interest diminished. In an effort to revitalize this program, Christian Education was replaced with Discipleship Hour (DH). A committee provides suggestions and oversight for the DH program. However, groups are self-formed around interest in a given subject and are usually small and discussion oriented. On occasion they can be quite large, especially if there is an outside speaker. To enhance group bonding, groups are encouraged to stay together for at least a year. Some have continued for unlimited periods. Several groups are now age based. Unfortunately, because of space problems, some of the groups meet in the sanctuary or other places that make group interaction more difficult.

One group—Sojourners—made up of ten couples ranging in age from the mid-fifties to the early eighties, has remained together since Discipleship Hour was established. They meet in a private home a few blocks from the church. They begin their session with prayer for the needs of each other and for the broader world. They have expanded their time together with occasional carry-in lunches and with cabin retreats. They choose their topics based on the interests and needs of the group.

Attendance in the adult Christian Education program was very high in the early years. In fact, at that time more people attended Sunday School than worship services. Today less than half of the adults participate in Discipleship Hour; although, there is some evidence of a recent increase in attendance.

One of the reasons that some people don't join a Discipleship Hour group is that they find their conversations during Coffee Hour to be more meaningful. However, some people don't enjoy the Coffee Hour or the Discipleship Hour. They either go home or to other places. Whether or not persons join a Discipleship Hour group continues to be a matter of concern. Not only does nonattendance conflict with our Statement of Expectations for members, it can create at times a we/they split between those who attend a group and those who do not. Many adults at AMC now question the relevance of Discipleship

Hour. Some persons who attend regularly can feel critical of those who don't. At the very least, the non-attenders miss an opportunity to bond with more people.

The other form of adult Christian Education is the Summer Bible School. An outside teacher is usually brought in from one of the seminaries or other institutions. Their teaching style is often formal and didactic. The content is sometimes based on a book they have written or on a subject for which they have special knowledge. The Bible School week starts on Sunday morning with a sermon by the guest teacher. The sessions are continued in the Discipleship Hour and for several of the following evenings. Traditionally the last session ends with an ice cream social. Over the years the level of input has been extraordinarily enriching. Unfortunately, a relatively small group of adults takes advantage of this event.

While the adults are meeting in their Bible School, the children also meet for their classes. Sometimes they follow a syndicated Summer Bible School curriculum. At other times they use the Marketplace 29 A.D. program that is built around activities that take place outside the building. The children are enthusiastic about Bible School and seem to benefit both socially and spiritually. However, their Bible School was cancelled in the summer of 2008 because of a decline in the number of children who were planning to attend and a lack of available leaders. Marketplace 29 A.D. is planned for 2009.

The children's Christian Education program has generally followed the curriculum of Herald Press. Throughout our history the children have been blessed with many gifted teachers, who, besides being effective at instruction, have been wonderful role models.

The teaching program for the MYF has been developed in various ways. In earlier years it tended to be centered on topical discussions that weren't specifically biblically based. However, some parents wanted a more explicit spiritual approach for their youth. That concern led to the hiring of our first Youth Pastor in 1982. It is interesting

"Marketplace 29 A.D.": Sam Wenger, instructor, 1996.

"Marketplace 29 A.D.": Jolene Weaver, Nicole Weaver, and Nancy Chapman, 2000.

Sunday School, grades 3 and 4: Don Ziegler, Matt Broaddus, and Brad Wyble, 1982.

to note that since that time more of the youth made faith commitments and became members.

The church has become more intentional in its effort to have the youth accept and follow Christ. The pastors form a Seekers Class every year and the youth are gently invited to make the choice that usually leads to baptism. They are encouraged to ask questions about faith and are given a number of months to process this most important decision. Their testimonies on the morning of their baptism are moving and tender. It can be a time of faith renewal for the adults.

Today the MYF curriculum is drawn from Anabaptist sources and sometimes from other places. However, it remains centered on faith development. The plan for the year is created by one of the co-pastors, although the youth and their advisors contribute actively in shaping the approach. It is processed at the annual fall retreat for the MYF and is tailored to meet the needs of each year's group.

Sunday School, grades 1 and 2: Maria Leister, Beth Douple, Andrea Buchen, and Dot Hershey, 1982.

Fifth grade Sunday School class, Bob Hurst, teacher; left to right: Kaylor Rosen-berry, Zachary Yoder, Julia Yoder, Annie Marie Wise, Meghan Nolt, and Amber Brubaker, 2008.

MYF—Row 3: Rachel Roth (Sawatsky), Jen Zimmerman (Stoltzfus), Eric Martin, Amy Martin (Burkholder), Becca Landis. Row 2: Anne Weaver, Margo Jantzi, Andrea Buchen (Foard), Colin Rupley (Rusel), Penn Miller, David Moyer, Jessica Landis. Row 1: Rose Jantzi, Beryl Jantzi, and Jonathan Penner, 1992.

The youth at AMC have been blessed over the years with many advisors who gave unselfishly to this very important mission. Of special note is Anne Weaver who served as a youth advisor longer than any person at AMC. She always did so with good humor, patience, and compassion. Even in this high-energy environment, Anne was unflappable and to this day continues to be a friend to many of the youth who came through the MYF during her time of service.

Library

As an adjunct to the Christian Education program at AMC, a library was started early in our history. It already had 300 volumes as well as other educational materials by 1964. It has grown steadily over the years and is used extensively by pastors, committees, and teachers. Additionally, parents can frequently be seen in the library with their

AMC Library: Beatrice Zorilla and Anna Clemens, 2009.

children, each taking an armload of books home for the next week. Various librarians have developed this very valuable resource.

The influence of Louise Leatherman is especially important. She guided the library for approximately thirty years and had a personal relationship with her collection and its users. The image of this former public school teacher behind the desk in the library carefully checking out books remains with us. She and the library were inseparable. Presently we have 4,497 books registered in the collection. Of that total 1,896 are for children. The library includes current AMC sermons, videos, and periodicals as well as the archives for the church.

ISSUES

No church is without controversy—including AMC. In our early years we experienced some tension over the requirement that women wear the devotional head covering during worship. We also had a concern about whether the wearing of wedding rings and other forms of jewelry was proper. After much discussion, we agreed to let members practice according to their convictions. We discouraged the growing of tobacco. The farmers who were growing it willingly discontinued this practice.

Now, nearly 50 years later these issues might seem quaint and hard to understand, especially for younger members. Surrounded as we are in Lancaster County with its many conservative Mennonites and Amish people, our youth can hardly imagine that at one point we were even *partially plain.* And with the anti-tobacco spirit that is prevalent in our present national culture, they might be surprised that some of our members had ever grown tobacco!

Later more difficult and substantive issues arose. Perhaps the most difficult one concerned the issue of divorce and remarriage. A brief statement on divorce was written in 1964 indicating a disapproval of this developing trend in the broader culture. At that time divorce within the broader Mennonite Church was almost nonexistent, but AMC apparently anticipated what might be coming.

It wouldn't be until 1971 that AMC would be confronted personally with divorce. Taken off guard, we attempted to be sensitive to the persons involved. However, the firmness that we showed in upholding our standard was offensive to the person who was leaving the marriage. Because of our disapproval, this person chose to withdraw from AMC.

Several years after this experience, a divorced woman who was married to an AMC member sought membership for herself. However, the congregation was still resistant to the idea of accepting divorce and remarriage. To deal more effectively with this issue, a Marriage Reconciliation Process Committee (MRPC) was formed to study the matter further and to develop guidelines. That process offended the applicant and she chose not to affiliate with AMC.

However, the MRPC recommended in 1979 that the congregation appoint a Divorce Reconciliation Committee (DRC) to deal more helpfully with the issue of divorce and remarriage. The DRC was asked to meet with anyone who was separating from their spouse to see if reconciliation could occur. Professional marriage counseling was recommended for some couples. In addition, the committee reviewed the applications for membership of persons who had been divorced and remarried. Among other things, the committee assessed the reasons for the marital failure and whether the person(s) seeking membership had asked for forgiveness for their part of the failure. They were also questioned about their relationship with God. The main goal of the committee was to prevent additional divorces.

By 1992, the pastors and the church leaders found this process to be cumbersome and offensive to some persons. The committee was then disbanded. Now marital problems are handled by pastors or referred to outside specialists. Persons applying for membership who are divorced and remarried are now considered on the same basis as other applicants.

Over the years various other issues have arisen within the congregation. Dual membership in both the Mennonite Church and the General Conference Mennonite Church created tension for a period of time, especially over how to fairly and proportionately support the programs of the separate denominations. That issue was resolved when the two denominations merged in 2002.

We experienced controversy briefly over the payment of war taxes. Several members who withheld a portion of their federal taxes needed a letter of support from AMC that would be sent to the IRS. Some members objected to having the church participate in this process.

The request by several families to have their preadolescent children baptized created a stir. The pastor at that time felt they were too young, but after much discussion the children were baptized. In a similar way, the church struggled with accepting the validity of baptism that an adult applicant for membership had received when he was an infant. He had grown up in South America and was baptized in his Catholic church. He resisted being rebaptized because he thought the second baptism would negate his original baptism. It was a painful time for him and the congregation although he was eventually accepted as a member without being rebaptized. Now some applicants choose to be rebaptized and some don't. The issue has lost some of its passion.

The issue of homosexuality has generated a degree of tension in recent years. Although the congregation has stated its support for the position of Mennonite Church USA, there are some members who believe that AMC should take a more proactive and welcoming stance on this issue. They formed a support group and have held a number of classes to invite dialogue. While there may never be complete agreement on homosexuality, the people with different opinions on this subject seem tolerant of each other.

SUMMARY

If it is true that AMC began its spiritual journey with a bit of a *cutting edge* or with a *rebel streak*, it might be fair to ask whether some of that image remains fifty years later. While we may still have vestiges of hubris, it is also clear that we are a community that has placed Christ in the center of our life. We are deeply committed to peace, justice, and simple living. Our level of stewardship of time and money remains extraordinarily high. We have struggled with tough issues and we have made sincere efforts to resist complete assimilation into the dominant culture. Although our most recent vision statement isn't in our conscious mind, it does direct our spirituality in subtle ways. Indeed, we are pilgrims on a sincere journey with each other—a journey that we believe attempts to follow in the footsteps of Christ.

Chapter Eight

Spiritual Leaders

Anabaptists have historically practiced *the priesthood of all believers.* Our denomination has resisted hierarchical forms of leadership, believing that members themselves needed to be involved in interpreting scripture and shaping practice. Even though we ordained pastors to be our spiritual leaders, we didn't want them to be too far apart from the membership. In our Anabaptist history, pastors have often been selected from within their congregations. Many of them have been bivocational. However, at AMC all but one of our pastors came from outside the congregation. In addition, since 1965 they have all been employed full-time by the congregation.

Although we still value the *shared priesthood* concept in theory, AMC has always called *professional* pastors to lead the congregation. We depend on them for their theological expertise; we expect them to be skillful in preaching, teaching, visitation, performing sacerdotal functions, and in counseling. Congregational polity requires, however, that laypersons conduct the business of the church and carry out its various programs. To that extent, we still practice the *priesthood of all believers* concept. While we expect our pastors to be *professionals,* we also want them to be *servant leaders.*

Throughout our fifty years, AMC has been blessed with many gifted pastors. The following is a brief narrative of the pastors and staff who have served us throughout our history.

PASTORS

GLENN ESH (1959-1961)

Our first pastor, Glenn Esh, divided his time between AMC and Monterey for about eighteen months. He was a convener, preacher, and a mentor during this fragile stage in our history. Although he was quite moderate in his spiritual practices, he wore a plain coat during the time he was our pastor. Indeed, most ministers in the (Old) Mennonite Church at that time wore plain coats. Because he was at AMC only part-time, he played a minimal role in defining our spiritual identity. He was, in a sense, an interim pastor.

The title of the first sermon preached for our new congregation was *If You Have Faith. (Colossians 1:1-8)* Just as the Apostle Paul was doing in his letter to the Colossians, Glenn was attempting to bring hope and courage to his new flock at the beginning of their journey.

Glenn graduated from Goshen College with a major in chemistry and worked for a brief time as a chemical engineer for Sylvania. He was drafted during World War II and served a term of alternative service as director of the CPS camps in Maryland and Virginia. After completing his obligations to Selective Service, he came to Akron to work at MCC. During that time Glenn took seminary classes and accepted a pastorate at the newly established Monterey Mennonite Church. He served there from 1948-1965. After leaving Monterey he spent several years as pastor of Neil Avenue Mennonite Church in Columbus, Ohio. He left the ministry to work in community service in Columbus. Glenn died in 2008 at the age of 89.

Glenn Esh, minister, 1959.

KERMIT DERSTINE (1961-1968)

Kermit Derstine became our pastor in August 1961. At first he was employed part-time, splitting his duties at AMC with an assignment at MCC. He became our full-time pastor in 1965. He was a 1959 graduate of the Mennonite Biblical Seminary in Goshen, Indiana (now AMBS in Elkhart, Indiana). Kermit expressed a cautious approach to the *world* as was common in the church at that time.

Kermit Derstine, minister, 1959.

He didn't want us to stray too far from our roots. Reflecting the challenges that came from the culture at that time, he presented a series of sermons about how to properly use the new invention—TV.

His sermons titles included: *Growth, Not Perfection; Before The Sermon Begins;* and *Partners With God.* Kermit gave encouragement to his young congregants who might still have been feeling some uncertainty on this new journey.

He helped us create a commitment statement that expected members to attend all services at the church and to become involved in one of the newly formed house church groups. We agreed to confront each other about perceived spiritual failures. We signed the commitment as a solemn promise to each other. What was different, though, was that we placed spiritual authority within the group, not entirely with the Pastor or the Bishop/Overseer. This early intensity about spiritual discipline weakened as the church grew larger and more tolerant of differences. Gradually the lines separating us from the *world* became less distinct.

Kermit Derstine was a reflective servant leader who walked softly on the virgin soil of a new church. It wasn't in his nature to exert authority unilaterally. Trying hard to avoid being a stereotypical Mennonite pastor, he took some liberties in redefining his role. But he heeded Bishop O. N. Johns' advice to not deliberately antagonize the Lancaster Conference neighbors, especially to not *proselytize* their members.

Kermit thoroughly believed in the *priesthood of all believers*. He requested that one member of the advisory group regularly review his preaching. He frequently asked members to preach. Early on he invited one of the young families to be a part of a worship service during Advent. They, with their young sons, introduced the Advent wreath with lit candles, a forerunner to our present Christ Candle. As the minister of a young congregation, Kermit was called on to officiate at the funerals of four children and three adults so early in our history. This was a stressful time for him and the congregation.

As a social activist, Kermit helped us to develop an awareness of needs in the broader community. He was instrumental in having the church create housing for a poor family in Lancaster. He also engaged the congregation with the needs of prisoners and the mentally ill. At this early stage he was surprisingly ecumenical and community focused.

His sermons were thoughtful, gentle, and somewhat unconventional. A charter member recalls that his approach to preaching was more topical in nature than driven by biblical texts. In that spirit, Kermit could also be prophetic, especially about political and societal issues. That worldview has continued to define AMC. Kermit remembered his time at AMC fondly and said he learned much from his time with us. In his words, he "thrived on our moments together."

After serving us for seven years, Kermit left to pastor a young church in Denver, Colorado. He was there for seven years and left the ministry at the age of 42. He had subsequent careers in real estate and in human services and died in 2008 at the age of 75.

Don Blosser (1969-1976)

AMC welcomed Don Blosser to serve as our pastor in July 1969. He was a graduate of the Associated Mennonite Biblical Seminary in Elkhart, Indiana. Don's sermons were hermeneutical in style, rapid-fire in delivery, and provocative politically and spiritually. His sermon titles were often put in question form. Generally he emphasized the importance of Jesus as Lord. Reflecting this belief some of his sermon titles were: *What Did Jesus Say About Killing People? (Matthew 5:21-26)* and *But What's Wrong With My Way? (Luke 2:41-52).*

Don Blosser, 1976.

While he was aware of the broader American culture of rebellion that was common in the late 1960s and 1970s, his pastoral style undoubtedly reflected his own beliefs. This was a time of unusual societal turbulence. The war in Vietnam, the Hippie movement, the widespread use of illicit drugs, the sexual revolution, protest marches, and other factors were inescapable for any pastor during that time. Don says, "My own faith went through dramatic growth as we (AMC) wrestled with important faith issues." Further, he says that both he and his wife Carolyn have positive memories of their years at AMC and of the many friendships they made while they were with us.

Don actively supported the continuation of house church groups and mission outreach. He was instrumental in starting two new offshoots of AMC. One of them, Pilgrims Mennonite Church, continues to meet. The other one, Donegal, doesn't. He was known as a good teacher. At times his methods of addressing issues created controversy within the congregation. His style of leadership could bring out divisions between members who were progressive and those who were conservative, especially in political areas. He encouraged animated discussions as a way of stretching people's thinking.

He wasn't particularly comfortable with the part of his pastoral role that required hospital visits or counseling. He resigned after being with us seven years to attend St. Andrews University in Scotland, where he received his Ph. D. Recognizing that his primary gifts and interests were in teaching, he accepted a position as a professor in the Bible Department at Goshen College upon completing his doctoral work. He retired from college teaching in 2001. Don had a subsequent career as a team leader at the Oakwood Christian Leadership Academy in Syracuse, Indiana.

TRUMAN BRUNK (1977-1985)

Truman Brunk, 1978.

Truman Brunk, Jr. came to AMC as pastor in September 1977 from Eastern Mennonite College where he had served as Campus Pastor for twelve years. While at EMC he completed his Masters of Divinity degree at Union Theological Seminary in Richmond, Virginia in 1969. Some of his former students at EMC would now be members in his new congregation. Indeed, he had officiated at the weddings of several of them.

His style as a pastor was noticeably different from that of his predecessors. While some of the previous pastors sometimes stretched the boundaries of Mennonite traditions, Truman appealed to the members to increase their personal relationships with God. Indeed he used more *God language*. To him, faith was something that could be *experienced* as much as *known*. In the tension between the head and the heart, Truman came out on the side of *heart*. Among some of his sermons were: *Disciplines of Love (I John 4:7-21); Knowing and Owning the Story (I John: 1-10);* and *Prayer, a Reflection of Life (Luke 18:1-14).*

Large in body and spirit, he brought with him Southern warmth and folksiness. He was informal in personality and quickly learned to know his members. He announced to the congregation at the beginning of his pastorate that he wanted to spend an hour with every member sometime during the year. For the most part he was able to accomplish that goal. He and his wife Betty formed a house church group in their home for newcomers at AMC and stayed with them until they were firmly established in the church.

While he was aware that some people might compare him with his evangelist uncle George Brunk, Jr., Truman was his own person. He was shaped more in the mold of his father Truman, Sr., who was a soft-spoken, mediation-type pastor in the Virginia Mennonite Conference. Truman had stage presence and charisma but shied away from excessive drama and from methods

Church Retreat: Truman Brunk and Nancy Rolon, 1981.

that could have, to some people, seemed emotionally manipulative. If anything, Truman's style was understated.

Despite skepticism from some members at AMC, Truman was able to bring back to the congregation a measure of meaningful piety and overt spirituality. During this time, more people began carrying their Bibles to church. His sermons were driven more by story than by hermeneutics. He related closely to the lives of the people in the congregation and brought a sense of energy and bonding to the community. His joyfulness, humor, and pathos were contagious. He had an unusual ability to discern and develop the gifts of members.

Theologically, he was moderate. He avoided being drawn into polarizing causes. While aware of national trends in the church and society, they didn't drive him. He frequently made references to the *Pentagon* that is within us as well as criticizing the defense headquarters in Washington, D.C.

As a former businessman, Truman was gifted in the administrative aspect of church life. While he was active in committees and congregational decision making, his leadership was always facilitative more than directive. He created the concept of the Pastoral Team—a group made up of the paid pastors and lay members. The lay members were given specific assignments and most importantly were a sounding board for his ministry.

After serving eight years, he left AMC to pastor the church of his birthplace, Warwick River Mennonite Church in Newport News, Virginia. Later he became Lead Pastor at Blooming Glen Mennonite Church in the Franconia Conference and then Associate Pastor at Harrisonburg Mennonite Church in Virginia. He then taught part-time at Eastern Mennonite Seminary and also served part-time as pastor for seminary students for one year. In his retirement years, he accepted several interim pastoral assignments. Together with Betty, he authored *That Amazing Junk Man* in 2007, a book of stories garnered from his years as a pastor.

BERYL JANTZI, YOUTH PASTOR (1982-1986)

During Truman's tenure at AMC, he and some of the youth leaders felt a need to have a pastor who could relate specifically to the youth of the church. Beryl Jantzi was called in 1982. Youthful at the age of 23, Beryl arrived after graduating from EMC and serving as a counselor at Beaver Camp in New York State. Guitar in hand and with fresh enthusiasm, he was assigned to this burgeoning sector of the church.

There was a growing concern that our youth needed a more intentional approach to their spiritual development. In the years prior

to Beryl's coming, the MYF program was
more activity centered and Sunday School
time was frequently spent on social issues
more than specifically on spiritual growth.
Strumming his guitar and teaching the
youth *camp songs* was no small challenge for
Beryl. Talking about the Bible wasn't any
easier. There was some initial resistance to
this new approach, but his winsome ways
paid off. There was a palpable change in
the spirituality of the youth that can still be
seen many years later. Beryl left AMC after
four years to take a position as associate pastor for youth at Warwick River Mennonite
Church in Newport News, Virginia.

Beryl Jantzi, 1982.

URBANE PEACHEY (1986-2000)

We didn't have to look very
far for our next Lead Pastor, Urbane
Peachey. He had served a year as interim pastor at AMC in 1976 and
was a lay member on the first Pastoral Team. He came to the position
with a Masters degree in Public and
International Affairs from the University of Pittsburgh (1972). While
pastoring at AMC, he was encouraged to pursue a Master of Divinity
degree and he completed that work
at the Lancaster Theological Semi-

Urbane Peachey, 1988.

nary in 1992. Later he studied part time at the Princeton Theological
Seminary, receiving a Masters in Theology degree with a specialty in
Pastoral Care and Counseling in 1998.

Urbane was our first pastor to be called from within the congregation. We knew him and he knew us. He needed little orientation but, as an *insider,* he wasn't afforded the *honeymoon* that is often given to pastors who come from outside the congregation. Because we knew him, we expected more from him from day one. Although he was in a new role with us, he was the same person that we had known previously.

From his experiences while living in the Middle East and from his study of various religious disciplines, Urbane introduced the church to new worship rituals, some of them described in Chapter seven. In his earlier years he invited us to kneel for prayer. That brought back memories from the childhood church experiences of some of us. He also taught us to receive the benediction with open eyes. Healing services and special remembrances on the one-year anniversary of a member's death were begun by Urbane. He loved music and sometimes sang in the choir, even on Sundays when he was preaching.

Because of his diverse background, Urbane brought to us a broad worldview. He made frequent references to multicultural stories and situations. He kept us firmly anchored in the peace and justice themes, drawing from his previous assignment in the Peace Section of MCC. His heart was in the international and national scene and that came through in his ministry.

His style of speaking was metaphorical and symbolic. It was important to stay focused on what he was saying. A break in concentration for the listener could make it hard to catch up with him later. Members who sought more literal language didn't always understand his more subtle points. Although his sermons might not have been fully comprehended by some listeners, few people criticized his intentions. Several of his sermon titles were: *And the Spirit of God Moves (Matthew 5:1-11)*; *Time, Culture, and Place (John 14:1-3)*; and *Sears Best Christianity.* These sermons reflect his attempts to have members grow spiritually and to apply new truths to the context they are a part of.

Urbane's sensitivity to the needs of members increased following the tragic loss of his oldest son Charles from an acute viral infection of the heart in 1989. Charles was twenty-eight at the time and was at the beginning of what surely could have been a full and rich life. Urbane and his family grieved that loss deeply. Somehow he was able to continue on as pastor through this most difficult time.

The most outstanding example of his sensitivity came in the spring of 1994 when the 15-year-old son of a member couple drowned in a nearby river. Urbane sat with the family on the bank of the river until the teen was recovered. He knew what it was like to experience loss. During his term of service, three other members would die prematurely. He served fourteen years until his retirement. He developed a counseling practice during his retirement.

FRED SWARTZENTRUBER, YOUTH PASTOR (1987-1989)

Fred Swartzentruber was called to be our youth pastor in 1987. He was a tall, gentle man who at times seemed shy and ill at ease in his assignment. His spirituality was never in question. He related well to some of the youth but there was a concern that he wasn't strong enough as a leader. Maybe we were expecting him to replicate Beryl Jantzi's skill and confidence. Perhaps we failed to give him the support and mentoring that he needed. Numerous attempts to help him grow were offered with no noticeable changes. It is likely that the assignment didn't match his skills.

Fred and Mina Swartzentruber, 1987.

Whatever the case, his termination after two years was one of the most controversial experiences at AMC. There was a deep divide within the congregation over whether he should stay or leave. A membership meeting held to discuss the matter shortly before he left was filled with acrimony. It took a long time for that wound to heal. Fred now says, "Reflecting on my experience as youth pastor at Akron, I think of the word *challenging*! I found it to be a real learning experience and a time for personal growth." Since leaving AMC, Fred has worked in construction and is now supervisor of maintenance and grounds at the Oaklawn Psychiatric Center in Elkhart, Indiana.

PAUL LONGACRE (1989-1991)

Following Fred's departure, Paul Longacre, an AMC member, served halftime as interim Associate pastor with responsibility for the youth. He was assigned to meet with the youth during Sunday School. He also preached occasionally and did some teaching of adult classes, visitation, and administration. He has good memories of the ways the youth interacted with him in Sunday School.

BERYL JANTZI (1991-1996)

Our former Youth Pastor, Beryl Jantzi, finished his seminary studies at Eastern Mennonite Seminary in 1991 and was called back to AMC to serve full time as associate pastor for both adults and youth. This *new and revised version* of Beryl was widely respected. His increased maturity, marital status, and seminary training made him valuable to the entire congregation.

Beryl, Margo, and Rose Jantzi, 1991.

His sermons revealed his youthful maturity. They were filled with a fresh and rather uncomplicated view of God. Instead of being deeply philosophical, they were common sense approaches to real life issues. Reflecting that he was now married and a father, Beryl had a new understanding of the adult, married world. An example of his style is shown in a sermon, *On Being Christian (Romans 12:1-2, 9-21)*. His spontaneity and energy were important to AMC at this critical time. He was especially important to young families, although he was widely respected by the entire congregation.

After five years Beryl left AMC to become Lead Pastor at Harrisonburg Mennonite Church in Virginia, where he served in that capacity for almost ten years He is currently the Mid-Atlantic Church Relations Manager for Mennonite Mutual Aid and also Moderator of the Virginia Conference. He states he is still actively involved in the life of the church even though he isn't in pastoral ministry. In reflecting on his time with us, he considers it "an honor to have been able to serve at AMC during the formative years" of his life.

NANCY HEISEY (1996)

Nancy Heisey served part time as Preaching Associate and Youth Director at AMC during the interim period between Beryl and the next pastor. Although she was the first woman to serve in this capacity, not much attention was given to the importance of this change. Her primary assignment was with the youth and her stay with us was known to be temporary. She was chosen on the strength of her overall gifts. Indeed, her contributions to the congregation were significant during her short time with us. Her sermons were clear and informative, perhaps reflecting the doctoral studies that she was pursuing at the time. Until recently, she has been President of the Mennonite World Conference. She is a professor in the Bible Department at EMU.

Dawn Yoder Harms (1997 to present)

Dawn Yoder Harms was invited in 1997 to serve AMC as our first, full time female pastor. Although she carries this unique role as pastor, a number of women at AMC have held meaningful assignments almost from the beginning of our church. The Advisory Committee welcomed its first female member in 1965. Doris Longacre served as our first female Congregational Chairperson in 1973. Later, Truman Brunk was intentional about using women to assist with worship, as members of the pastoral team, and in other meaningful roles.

Pastor Dawn Yoder Harms, 2009.

Pastoral Team: John Hostetler, Marilyn Langeman, Nancy Chapman, Dawn Yoder Harms and Jim Amstutz, 2002.

From the beginning of her time at AMC, Dawn has divided her time between the adults and the youth. She had not yet completed her studies at the Associated Mennonite Biblical Seminary in Elkhart, Indiana, when she arrived. The congregation was so enthusiastic about her that she was offered the opportunity to complete her Seminary work—which she did in 1999—while serving as our associate pastor. With her obvious gifts and the fact that she was here full time, it was clear that the female voice would be raised to a new level. She has presented herself with humility and with a genuine sense of spiritual mission. She has been aware of her uniqueness as a woman pastor but hasn't made that her *imprimatur.*

Dawn had extensive experience with MCC in Portugal, Congo/Zaire, and Appalachia before accepting this assignment. She has continued the AMC tradition of being sensitive to other countries and other cultures. Dawn makes frequent references to poverty and encourages us to reach out to others in acts of service. Her sermons are thoughtful and hermeneutically thorough as she tells the biblical story. She precedes her sermons with a modified version for the children who assemble with her in the front of the sanctuary for the children's story. This gives them a better understanding of the sermon that is to come. It also serves as a preparation for the adults who hear the theme twice.

Her approach to scripture and life is Christ-centered. Often her sermons have personal applications for members. Some of the titles were *Seek King Jesus (Matthew 2:1-12)*, *I Do Choose (Mark 1:40-45)*, and *Love Light Darkness (Jeremiah 33:14-16, Luke 21:25-36)*. She emphasizes the importance of asking questions and of finding God in times of trial. Dawn occasionally surprises the congregation by reciting from memory the passage of scripture upon which her sermon is based. She delivers the scripture in a dramatic fashion, almost as if she were the writer.

Increasingly her time is being spent in pastoral care and visitation. She adds an important perspective to the counseling sessions.

When visiting elderly members, she occasionally takes her autoharp along to enrich the visits. She is also a talented drummer and pianist. Because of her responsibilities with the youth, she is less accessible in the foyer following the worship services. She presently serves as co-pastor. Dawn announced her resignation on March 10, 2009. She will end her time with us in December 2009.

JIM AMSTUTZ (2001 TO PRESENT)

Jim Amstutz was called to AMC as Lead Pastor in July 2000. At that time he was serving as pastor of the West Swamp Mennonite Church, some 60 miles to the east. The affirmation for his coming was so strong that we waited until August 2001 for him to join us. That allowed him to complete his commitment to WSMC.

We had already known Jim because he had been a member here between 1991-1994 while he was work-   *Pastor James S. Amstutz, 2009.*
ing at the MCC headquarters. Before that he was Campus Pastor at Bluffton College (now University) in Bluffton, Ohio. He was also the men's soccer coach. Jim is a 1987 graduate of AMBS with an M. Div. degree. He began a Doctor of Ministry program at the Fuller Theological Seminary in Pasadena, California in 2003. Part of his academic work could be done in Akron, but occasionally he needed to be on campus at Fuller. He received the D. Min. degree in 2008.

Jim is, at the core, a scholar and teacher. His sermons are primarily hermeneutical in style and relate directly to the chosen text for the morning. His knowledge of scripture and his ability to interpret given texts is unusual. The sermons are thorough explanations of the cultural context in which the Scriptures are based. His style of delivery is didactic but is occasionally accompanied with passion for the needs of the poor and homeless, as well as other issues regarding peace and justice. Several of his sermon titles have been: *Do You Want to be Well?* (*John 5:1-9*); *The Spirit Gives Strength* (*Acts 6:8-15, 9:54-81*); and *The Limbs of Angels* (*Matthew 2:13-23*).

He presents with a sense of calm and dignity. Much like Kermit Derstine, Jim is very involved in reaching out to persons in need in the broader community. He serves on various ecumenical committees in the county, including Homes of Hope.

Jim is embedded in the administrative functions of AMC. He has a deep interest in the way the church runs, takes a hands-on approach with committees and in the governance functions of the church. His guiding instrument in leading the congregation is Appreciative Inquiry, a method that emphasizes building congregational mission from its strengths rather than by getting sidetracked with its weaknesses.

Jim asked in 2004 that he and Dawn change their titles to *co-pastor* to better reflect their roles. His responsibilities continue to change as needs within the congregation present themselves. He has recently begun to give leadership to a young parents group at AMC and is increasing his pastoral visits with members.

CHURCH SECRETARY/ADMINISTRATOR

For several years we had a part-time secretary who prepared the bulletin and typed letters for the pastor. As the congregation grew, the title of the position was changed to Administrative Assistant to reflect its broader function. The title was again changed in 1996 to Church Administrator. It then became a full-time position. These changes were necessary because of increasing membership and the growing complexity of running the church office. It is a hub of activity with members stopping in, the phone ringing, emails being exchanged, reports processed, and it is where staff and leaders check in. On occasion, staff members from DSECC also stop by with questions or needs.

For the last several decades, the people holding this position have played a role in decision making at AMC. They have been important in carrying out the administrative functions of the church. The current administrator Janet Weber serves as a resource to the various church committees, including the Congregational Council. She receives and archives their reports and informally assures that their func-

Janet Weber, 2009.

tions are implemented. The administrator works closely with the Church Chair and Pastors in setting agenda for the Council. She also coordinates the finances of the church under the supervision of the Church Treasurer and handles the scheduling of church facilities. When problems arise within the building or on the grounds, the Administrator notifies the Trustees who then arrange for repairs. Janet Weber has served very effectively in this capacity since 2000. During her time, a volunteer developed a web site—*www. akronmench.org.*

MUSIC MINISTER

Marcella Hostetler was hired in 1991 on a quarter-time basis as our first Music Minister. She served until 1992 when she left to take another assignment. An AMC member, Cheryl Eshleman, was hired on a half-time basis to replace her, and because the congregation benefited from her additional time, the position has remained half time ever since. After four years Cheryl resigned to attend to her growing family. Larry Penner replaced Cheryl in 1996 for two years. When he left in 1998 to accept a full-time position elsewhere, he was replaced by Mary Ann Johnson who served for four years. Patricia Martin has served as our Music Minister since 2002.

Patricia Martin, 2009.

Each of these musicians brought with them their own style and personality. All of them enriched the life of AMC. They were responsible for the music programs for both children and adults. In addition, they coordinated with the pastors the music themes for the morning worship. From time to time, each developed and led special music programs. They invited people from the congregation to form and lead various music groups, although some of those groups were in place before and functioned independently from the leadership of the Music Minister.

CHILDREN'S EDUCATION MINISTER

Reflecting a strong growth in the number of children within the congregation, AMC member Mary Jane Crockett was hired in 1999 as Children's Education Minister. This

Mary Jane Crockett, 1999.

has been a half-time assignment. She coordinates the curriculum selection and teacher assignments. She is also responsible for the scheduling and implementation of the Summer Bible School. Mary Jane remains in this position.

MINISTER OF PASTORAL CARE

From September 2007 through December 2008, Jeanette Bontrager served as a Minister of Pastoral Care. This quarter-time position was created primarily to attend to the needs of the very large cohort of members over sixty-five and to care for other members who were experiencing various health problems. As a nurse she used her professional skills during her visits with members who were in the hospital and during their recovery time at home. She was a valuable adjunct to the Pastors. She resigned this position to return to her previous job as school nurse in Ephrata.

STUDENT INTERNS

Throughout our history we have been a training center for persons exploring ministry as a calling. Most were studying at the various seminaries, including AMBS in Elkhart, Indiana. A few were still college students and were in the Ministry Inquiry Program to assist younger persons in knowing whether pastoral ministry matched their skills and interests. These students have enriched our lives. A list of these students is in the appendix.

VOLUNTEER LEADERS

As a group who believes in the *priesthood of all believers,* AMC has been a vital congregation because of all the volunteer leaders who have given large amounts of time to serve the church. These volunteers have served as Sunday School teachers, committee members, Congregational Council members, treasurers, trustees, mentors, youth advisors, and in a host of other leadership positions. Some of them will also be noted in the appendix. Space limits make it impossible to name them all. However, special attention needs to be drawn to Glenn Weaver who has given unlimited amounts of time as treasurer as well as serving on numerous finance and building committees. His ability to see the big financial picture has been remarkable. His son Mark is following in his father's footsteps. AMC has been well led.

Chapter Nine

Pilgrims' Progress: Lessons From the Journey

Our 50-year pilgrimage is a story of the *people* who have walked this journey together as well as a story of our *congregation*—Akron Mennonite Church. Church histories are of necessity about individuals *and* the congregations of which they are a part. Just as individuals have distinct personalities, so do their congregations. To varying degrees they give shape to each other. Both are dynamic, living organisms with identifiable and unique characteristics—some expressed as strengths and some as challenges.

All individuals, as well as congregations, have some of both. It is important to name them—to celebrate and build on the strengths and to meet the challenges that face us. First, a look at some of the strengths present at AMC over the years:

COMMITMENT TO AN ANABAPTIST UNDERSTANDING OF SCRIPTURE

When we started our journey in 1959, we were intentionally positioned within the Anabaptist tradition. We have never wavered from that position. All of the charter members had grown up in Mennonite congregations. From our beginning, the connection with the Anabaptist identity was strengthened through our involvement with many of the Mennonite organizations, especially MCC. Indeed, that organization was indirectly responsible for the formation of AMC. Many of their staff members have been members of our congregation and many of its volunteers have worshipped with us. This connection with MCC—and indeed with various church agencies—has cemented our bond with the broader Anabaptist vision.

Central in that theology is Menno Simons' strong emphasis on following Christ in all of life—every day of the week. Part of that call is to be committed to peace and justice. We have also tried to live simply and avoid materialism. We have accepted the invitation to live as servants in our community and to each other. We advocate the concept of the *priesthood of all believers* and are diligent about avoiding hierarchy in church life.

Commitment to a Progressive Faith

In the early years, AMC was a comfortable place for Mennonites coming to the area from other communities. Some of us were employees of MCC. Increasingly, new members came to the community to practice professions or to establish businesses. Others transferred their membership from Lancaster Conference churches and were seeking a different church experience. Many of them had been exposed to different kinds of practices while they were in college or serving terms of alternative service assignments in other communities. Some of the incoming members were attracted to AMC because of its acceptance of divorce and remarriage. For a variety of reasons many of us came to AMC because it was compatible with our understanding of Christian practice.

Commitment to Mission

Mission has been a part of our identity from the very beginning. We have a long history of providing housing to the homeless and the poor. We have always responded to calls for help at the sites of natural disasters. We send food to the hungry and support the programs of MCC and other church agencies. We are a church of volunteers who visit people in prisons and hospitals. We serve on crisis hot lines. And we have been instrumental in founding numerous health and welfare agencies. We have played a key role in settling refugees in our community. Many of us have served overseas or in disadvantaged areas in our own country. We give selflessly locally, nationally, and internationally as board members. We have been present at places of international conflict, giving a Christian witness of peace and justice.

COMMITMENT TO LEADERSHIP

AMC has been blessed with a large number of leaders, many with high levels of formal education and professional training. Some are entrepreneurs who create businesses and products, and some have been financial experts. Several are scientists who led significant national projects. A few have been theologians who have written extensively. AMC has had many published authors, some with widespread reputations. We are the educators of students—in settings ranging from day care through graduate school. Sometimes we are their principals. We are physicians and health care workers. Many of us have gifts that are expressed behind the scenes.

COMMITMENT TO STEWARDSHIP

We have a long and unwavering commitment to the stewardship of our resources. In these fifty years, we have always met our budget. In every year but the present one, our giving budget has increased. We have been intentional about directing generous portions of our budget to causes outside the congregation. We also support other worthy projects both within and outside the congregation independent of the budget. In this same spirit we have attempted to be good stewards of the environment and of our physical resources.

COMMITMENT TO MUTUAL SUPPORT

AMC has done well over the years in giving support to members in crises. We have reached out to people who are sick, to those who are grieving the loss of family members, people who are experiencing financial difficulties, and for many others with physical, emotional, and spiritual needs. Some of the support has come from pastors, some from house church groups, and some from individual friendships. Practical expressions, such as providing meals, mowing yards, repairing houses, and giving advice about cars and finance, have revealed evidence of *bearing each other's burdens*.

COMMITMENT TO CREATIVITY

There is a rich history at AMC in supporting the creativity of its members. Our vocal and instrumental musicians continue to give color and meaning to the congregation. Younger children are frequently called on to contribute to worship. That same creativity is also evident in the visual arts produced by members. Wall hangings, pottery, and table arrangements give life to a somewhat stark building. In the past we staged a number of musicals and plays. For several years we held congregational retreats that were very meaningful and enriching. Teachers at all levels of the Christian Education program have been models of creativity for their students. The diversity of elective classes for adults during Discipleship Hour has been appealing to many people.

COMMITMENT TO THE NURTURE OF CHILDREN AND YOUTH

The children and youth of AMC have an opportunity to connect with adults in a variety of ways. Most are through structured mentoring programs. Some of these connections have led to long-term friendships between the child and the adult. These activities create a setting for support, listening, and teaching. This kind of support is also available through the advisors in the Junior MYF and in the MYF. One fairly new form of mentoring has been happening in the MYF Quiz Teams. This intensely competitive activity is not only a way for youth to learn Scripture, but is also a way for the coaches to mentor and for the students to form meaningful relationships.

This summarizes some of the strengths of AMC over the past 50 years. Others could have been identified. Indeed we have much to celebrate as we pause to reflect on our past. However, it is also important to look at some of the challenges that confront us as we move forward. No congregation can rest on its laurels or expect to remain in stasis. We must respond to the challenges that come from changes that are inevitable in every congregation. We also must respond to unresolved challenges from our past. The following are some of those challenges:

RESPONDING TO OUR IMAGE

From our beginning, some people have said that the personality of AMC revealed a *rebel spirit*. If that attitude has been present, has it defined who we are? Rebels can be contentious and can display an air of hubris. Rebels are often more driven by what they *oppose* than by what they *propose*. Their energy can be diverted away from being constructive and proactive, and into being more critical and oppositional.

We have also been described as *cutting edge*. To some observers that has meant we were unconventional and maybe even unorthodox. Over the years, we have stated that we value raising questions more than searching for answers. We don't like authority that is expressed too boldly. It has also been said that AMC has an attitude of superiority. We can be intimidating to some persons.

RESPONDING TO OUR EMOTIONAL SELF

Another aspect that has been identified in our congregational personality is that we don't seem to be comfortable displaying emotions—especially during our worship services. With some notable exceptions, we are usually contained in the ways we express emotions. If that is true, is that a byproduct of being more analytical and rational? Do we believe that ideas, concepts and formal statements are more appropriate than expressing ourselves through feelings? Efforts to have us loosen up during worship can be resisted. We have been known to *clap with one hand.* Visiting choirs or preachers from more expressive traditions can find us hard to engage emotionally.

RESPONDING TO OUR MONOCULTURE

Historically AMC has, for the most part, been made up of people who came from a white, middle class, and Swiss/German/Russian Mennonite background. That has changed very little over the years. A few members have Spanish and Eastern European surnames and there has been a slight increase in the number of members coming from other denominations. But, for the most part, we remain ethnically and racially much as we were in our beginning.

Our distance from urban centers can be an impediment to more diversity. For the most part, the Borough of Akron is similar to our church in its makeup. Many of our members have a broad worldview, but our monoculture at AMC is significant. Has that diminished our congregational life and limited our vision? It has always been difficult to know how to reach out to persons who are different from us. Maybe we are intentionally a niche church and are most comfortable being among people who are more like us.

RESPONDING TO GROWTH

Throughout our history we have been uneasy about numerical growth. We never actively sought new members. Perhaps because of the uniqueness of our congregation new members found us on their own. Over the years we have grown dramatically. By the standards described by the Alban Institute, we quickly moved from being a small *Pastoral* church to being a large *Program* church. For most of our existence, we have depended heavily on programs to meet our needs. While pastors have been vital for preaching and visitation, they have also been important in supporting lay leaders and committees and in setting the spiritual tone of the congregation. However, lay members largely maintain our infrastructure.

In recent years our attendance at worship has begun to slip. The challenges that come from being a large congregation remain. Some long-time members feel lost in the crowd and new persons can be overlooked. We don't know each other as well as we would like and we lament our lack of connection with each other. The ambivalence about size may be one reason we have resisted adding onto our building. Having inadequate space for fellowship meals and for Discipleship Hour classes continue to be issues.

Responding to Change

As is often the case with middle-aged institutions, we can find change to be difficult—whether it is in our building decisions, changing the order of the morning service, the style of our worship, maintaining the coffee hour in its present time slot, or even in the ways we make decisions. We don't seem to wander far from our comfort zone. But middle-aged institutions—whether restaurants or churches—need new *menus*. They may even have to rearrange the *furniture*. Change can be growth producing. Maintaining the status quo can create lethargy.

Responding to Governance Needs

As we have grown in size, it has been difficult to find the best mechanisms to govern ourselves. In the beginning we were small enough to make decisions as a group. Within the first decade, our growth forced us to use institutional models of governance. Responsibility for running the church was delegated to an appointed group. However, as that happened, members became more detached from the decision-making process. Their absence at membership meetings left them even farther from decision making. In addition, the effectiveness of the governing council has been hampered, to some extent, by the short terms of its members. Institutional memory has been lost in this process. The church record indicates that some important issues have been recycled and not resolved, perhaps because of this lack of continuity.

RESPONDING TO CHANGES IN THE MEANING OF MEMBERSHIP AND ATTENDANCE

Increasingly, the meaning of membership has lost some of its importance. Some members live in this community and rarely attend worship services at AMC, while some attend other churches and fail to transfer their church letters. Still others have moved to other communities but have kept their membership at AMC. Attempts to cull the membership list are often met with resistance. Sometimes it is by members themselves who want to keep connected with AMC. More often the resistance has been from their parents. The parents' fear is that removing their son or daughter from membership might affect them adversely.

This attitude about membership reflects a national trend in our denomination and in other churches. The implications of this practice are large. Among other things, it has become difficult to know who *belongs* to AMC. In addition to the lack of certainty about membership, the commitment to regular attendance at worship—even by more active members—has also declined. That, too, reflects a national trend. It is hard to know what programs are needed, and how to staff congregations when it is not clear how many people are to be served.

This uncertainty about who is and who is not affiliated with AMC can be an impediment to congregational cohesion. It is hard to bond with people who are on the margins. While this is a national phenomenon, it may be even more prevalent in our congregation. Indeed, over the years we have had a significant amount of turnover in our membership. Some of that has been by people affiliated with service agencies, especially MCC. We are a congregation that is on the go, including many who travel for their jobs. AMC has also been a temporary stopping off place for people who are church shopping. In this environment, some members can easily slip to the edges and be overlooked.

RESPONDING TO CHANGING DEMOGRAPHICS

The demographics at AMC are changing. Most of us at AMC are middle-aged or older. We are not being replaced by sufficient numbers of young persons. We need their leadership and their fresh ideas. We are no longer the main refuge for new people transferring in from other congregations or for persons who desire a progressive church. For most of our history we were unique, but we no longer are. Surrounded by a smorgasbord of congregations from which people can choose, we are now just one of many. In addition, the Mennonite *brand* isn't as important to some people as it once was.

As the congregation itself has aged, the *cutting edge* that we had earlier is now less sharp. Our creative energies have diminished. Middle-aged congregations often rest on their laurels and traditions. Maintenance often becomes the strategic plan more than growth and change. Have we become tired Pilgrims? Many of us have been on this long journey. Nevertheless, we have accomplished remarkable things on the way.

AT MILE MARKER 50: PILGRIMS' PROGRESS

Akron Mennonite Church has been a *light on a hill* from its beginning. That light has *not* gone out. We are still a committed people who are strong. For many years we have been energized by our youthfulness. Now we need to intentionally pass the torch to younger members who are the key to the future of AMC. Building on the strengths of the congregation, we can put new energy into finding answers for the challenges that lie ahead.

Indeed, the call to follow Christ in life is as important today as it was 50 years ago—and just as it was in Menno Simons' time. This journey is not yet over. New travelers will join the pilgrims who are a part of this journey. Responding to the call of hymn 307 in our *Worship Book* we will *walk the mile and bear the load* of fellow travelers. As we follow Christ, we will continue to serve each other and will never lose sight of the needs of the broader world. This is who Akron Mennonite Church was on October 4, 1959. It is who we are today. With God's guidance this is how we hope to be in the future. Indeed, the journey will continue!

Appendix

CHARTER MEMBERS

1. Menno Diener
2. Savilla Diener
3. Ura Gingerich
4. Gladys Gingerich
5. Earl Smoker
6. Vera Smoker
7. Paul Leatherman
8. Loretta Leatherman
9. Warren Leatherman
10. Louise Leatherman
11. Glenn Weaver
12. Anne Weaver
13. Earl Bowman
14. Irma Bowman
15. Albert Miller
16. Esther Miller
17. Edward Miller
18. David Hess
19. Ruth Hess
20. Edgar Stoesz
21. Gladys Stoesz
22. Clarence Brubaker
23. Grace Brubaker
24. Richard Weber
25. Viola Weber
26. Lester Weber
27. Lydia Weber
28. Robert Martin
29. Alverta Martin
30. John Hostetler
31. Kathy Hostetler
32. James Millen
33. Joy Millen
34. Anna Myers
35. Robert Miller
36. Jean Miller
37. Melvin Lapp
38. Virginia Lapp
39. Marlin Keens
40. Emma Keens
41. Willard Roth
42. Alice Roth
43. Merrill Raber
44. Beulah Raber
45. J.N. Byler
46. Edna Byler

a list of the entire membership available upon request

Deaths of Members and Attenders

1.	Cindy Voth	(child)	12/23/1959
2.	Suzanne Carper Miller	(infant)	04/10/1960
3.	J.N. Byler		04/14/1962
4.	Charlene Peachey	(child)	06/21/1962
5.	Ruth Wagner		03/18/1964
6.	Yvonne Hackman	(infant)	04/20/1968
7.	Emma Schlichting		07/23/1968
8.	Peter Neufeld	(infant)	12/05/1968
9.	Edna Ruth Byler		07/07/1976
10.	Alvin P Burgin		05/16/1979
11.	Joyce Moyer		07/20/1979
12.	Doris Longacre		11/10/1979
13.	Edward Lopez		04/29/1980
14.	James Hallman		10/10/1980
15.	Jed Roggie	(infant)	0 6/25/1982
16.	Loretta Leatherman		03/20/1983
17.	Orie Wolf		06/06/1986
18.	Clarence Brubaker		06/14/1987
19.	Charles Peachey		04/09/1989
20.	David Kurtz		08/06/1990
21.	Mary Beth Bowman Moser		08/26/1991
22.	Carson Glick		09/23/1991
23.	Maralee Strom		04/03/1992
24.	Melvin Lapp		01/21/1993
25.	Megan Marie Thalheimer	(infant)	03/23/1993
26.	Jonathan Lapp	(youth)	04/02/1994
27.	Ura Gingerich		01/05/1995
28.	Albert W Miller		01/28/1996
29.	Robert W Miller		06/17/1996
30.	Ronald A Moyer		01/27/1997

31. Robert Summers   08/30/1997
32. Kurt Ott   10/23/1997
33. Esther Miller   11/22/1997
34. Paul Miller   03/03/1998
35. Paul E Weaver, Jr.   04/30/1998
36. Savilla T Diener   04/19/1999
37. Rebecca Jayne Wanner   (stillborn)   02/16/2000
38. Grant Noll   03/03/2002
39. Jim Drescher   12/30/2002
40. Arthur A Voth   05/22/2003
41. Harriet Douple   06/07/2004
42. Rollin Rheinheimer   02/08/2005
43. Arianna Puljek-Shank   (infant)   02/01/2005
44. Susan Elaine Voth   05/11/2005
45. Daniel Valverde   09/20/2005
46. Michael Pugh   06/02/2006
47. Bertha Miller   06/13/2006
48. Leon Buckwalter   09/17/2006
49. Frances Nussbaum   03/21/2007
50. Esther Horst   04/09/2007
51. Sandra Lowery   06/13/2007
52. Louise Leatherman   08/20/2007
53. Robert D Buckwalter   11/30/2007
54. Clayton Martin   02/04/2008
55. Kris Yelk   04/10/2008
56. Eric Habegger   10/01/2008
57. Irene Martin   01/13/2009
58. Kathy Hostetler   03/28/2009

CONGREGATIONAL CHAIRPERSONS

Paul Leatherman	1959-1964
Lester Weber	1964-1965
Robert W Miller	1965-1967
Urbane Peachey	1967-1969
Paul Leatherman	1969-1970
Edgar Stoesz	1970-1973
Doris Longacre	1973-1977
John Grasse	1977-1979
Paul Leatherman	1979-1980
Gerald Kaufman	1980-1985
Herman Bontrager	1985-1988
Jerry Shank	1988-1991
Paul Longacre	1991-1994
Jim Smucker	1994-1999
Lynette Meck	1998-2000
Naomi Wyble	2000-2002
Lowell Detweiler	2002-2004
Bruce McCrae	2004-2005
Bob Wyble	2005-2008
Dale Hershey	2007-2009

TREASURERS

Albert Miller	1959-1961
Glenn Weaver	1962-1966
Robert Peifer	1967-1968
John Hostetler	1968-1970
Paul Myers	1970-1971
Seth Ebersole	1971-1975
Cal Britsch	1975-1977
Robert Peifer	1977-1978
Paul Longacre	1978-1981
Ken Langeman	1981-1985
Paul Myers	1985-1987
Ken Graber	1987-1989
Tim Classen	1989-1992
Robert Peifer	1992-1994
Mark Weaver	1995-1999
Ken Langeman	1999-2001
Robert Peifer	2001-2004
Ken Langeman	2004-2007
Mark Weaver	2007-2009

Secretaries/Administrators

Kathy Hostetler	1961-1969 + 1974-1978	secretary
Marti King	1978-1981	secretary/coordinator
Jean Buchen	1981-1984	secretary/coordinator
Marilyn Langeman	1984-1987	secretary/coordinator
Dawn Petticoffer Oswald	1987-1990	secretary/coordinator
Bonnie Hutchinson	1990-1991	secretary/coordinator
Julie Miller Zimmerman	1991-1996	administrative assistant
Melissa Roth	1996-2000	church administrator
Janet Weber	2000-present	church administrator

Secretaries Assisting the Office:

Esther Hostetter	1987
Marge Ruth	1995-1999
Jolene Weaver	1999-2006
June Landis	2004-present
Charity Shenk	2006-present

Pastoral Team - Lay Members

YEAR	TEAM MEMBER	TEAM MEMBER	TEAM MEMBER
1982	Urbane Peachey	Norma Johnson	
1983	Urbane Peachey	Norma Johnson	
1984	Gerry Raber	Norma Johnson	
1985	Gerry Raber	Urbane Peachey	
1986	Gerry Raber	Urbane Peachey	
1987	Marlene Kaufman	John Hostetler	
1988	Marlene Kaufman	John Hostetler	
1989	Marlene Kaufman	Ruth Detweiler	Elvin Stoltzfus
1990	Gloria Nussbaum	Ruth Detweiler	Elvin Stoltzfus
1991	Gloria Nussbaum	Ruth Detweiler	Elvin Stoltzfus
1992	Gloria Nussbaum	Ruth Detweiler	Dale Hershey
1993	Jeanette Bontrager	Linda Helmus	Dale Hershey
1994	Jeanette Bontrager	Linda Helmus	Dale Hershey
1995	Jeanette Bontrager	Linda Helmus	Nina Harnish
1996	Jeanette Bontrager	Jerry Shank	Nina Harnish
1997	Donna Shenk	Jerry Shank	Nina Harnish
1998	Donna Shenk	Jerry Shank	John Weber
1999	Donna Shenk	Nancy Chapman	John Weber
2000	Marilyn Langeman	Nancy Chapman	John Weber
2001	Marilyn Langeman	Nancy Chapman	John Hostetler
2002	Marilyn Langeman	Nancy Chapman	Dwight Yoder
2003	Dot Hershey	Nancy Chapman	Dwight Yoder
2004	Dot Hershey	Nancy Chapman	Richard Weaver
2005	Dot Hershey	Marilyn Wanner	Richard Weaver
2006	Patrice Flaming	Andres Zorrilla	Richard Weaver
2007	Patrice Flaming	Andres Zorrilla	Anne Weaver
2008	Patrice Flaming	Lloyd Kuhns	Anne Weaver
2009	Karyn Nancarvis	Lloyd Kuhns	Anne Weaver

Seminary/College Interns

Calvin King	1969-1970
Lorne Friesen	1971
Linda Schmidt	1992
Roger Farmer	1992
Nancy Heisey	1992-1993
Linda Helmus	1998
Rachel Roth	1998
Eli Passage	2006
Betsy Headrick McCrae	2006-2007

CONTRIBUTIONS 1960-2008

YEAR	MEMBERSHIP	CONTRIBUTION
1959	Started the year with $3,339 transferred from Monterey Mennonite Church	
1960	46	$18,465
1961	59	7,553
1962	82	28,040
1963	92	95,216
1964	99	24,389
1965	119	27,389
1966	137	30,168
1967	154	34,526
1968	162	33,330
1969	171	34,019
1970	180	40,516
1971	186	43,929
1972	199	49,413
1973	208	70,751
1974	227	63,812
1975	237	79,372
1976	245	81,987
1977	256	84,218
1978	267	114,900
1979	274	113,088
1980	293	150,075
1981	307	152,470
1982	313	184,000
1983	322	194,460
1984	339	203,770
1985	345	243,660

YEAR	MEMBERSHIP	CONTRIBUTION
1986	332	214,980
1987	347	601,390
1988	342	927,940
1989	340	777,039
1990	347	391,056
1991	356	412,514
1992	365	437,280
1993	373	438,604
1994	380	455,696
1995	388	490,966
1996	383	490,978
1997	401	481,193
1998	400	500,782
1999	399	503,763
2000	414	589,092
2001	417	610,884
2002	444	574,769
2003	445	583,759
2004	450	550,504
2005	453	616,420
2006	463	662,402
2007	466	614,826
2008	466	638.638

TIMELINE

DATE	ACTIVITY
October 4, 1959	First Sunday morning service – Brownstown Fire Hall; 89 persons present. Glenn Esh, pastor of Monterey Mennonite Church, served concurrently as AMC pastor until August 1961.
April 3, 1960	First Membership Commitment Statement
May 8, 1960	46 charter members received to form the official body of Akron Mennonite Church
October 1960	The Oberholtzer tract of 13 ½ acres was selected and purchased for $13,500.
August 1961	Kermit Derstine came to us as a licensed minister. He was ordained July 29, 1962, and served us for 7 years until 1968.
1962	The 13 ½ tract was annexed into the Borough of Akron in order to obtain water.
Sept.16, 1962	Groundbreaking ceremonies were held. Construction of the first stage was completed June 1963. Total cost of land, building and furnishings was $105,000.
June 14-16, 1963	Dedication of Akron Mennonite Church; membership was 92.
1963	Formation of House Churches
Sept. 8, 1964	Formation of Akron MYF
1969	WMSC volunteers with Community Action Program, Ephrata, with transportation and childcare.

DATE	ACTIVITY
1969	Diamond Street Nursery School for 4-year-olds began as a missions project.
April 1969	Dauphin Street house project in Lancaster was begun.
July 1969	Don Blosser became our pastor and served us for 7 years until 1976.
1969-1970	Pastoral internship for Calvin King, Goshen, Indiana.
August 1970	Head Start teaching program began, using two double rooms and the kitchen.
June 25, 1972	AMC was incorporated as a nonprofit corporation.
1972	AMC purchased house and land at the nearby Martin's pretzel factory at a public auction. The house was used for church office, MYF and Sunday school classes for about 5 years and was sold when the AMC addition was completed.
1973	Sponsorship of two Ugandan families–Sumar and Jiwa families.
August 1974	AMC accepted as a dual conference member of the General Conference Mennonite Church.
1974-1976	Jim Drescher was appointed as Church-Community worker for Akron/Ephrata area.
May 1976 - Feb.1977	Church facilities were enlarged to accommodate growing attendance–cost $150,000.
1976-1977	Urbane Peachey served as Interim Pastor.

DATE	ACTIVITY
1977	Formation of Pilgrims Mennonite Church
May 1977	Dedication of new addition; membership was 252.
September 1977	Truman Brunk became our Pastor and served us for 8 years until 1985.
June 1978	AMC Pictorial Directory was produced.
Sept. 17, 1978	Action was taken to develop a cemetery on AMC property.
November 1978	Atlantic Coast Conference established; AMC became a member.
1979	Sponsorship of Thun Ngo family
1979	Purchased piano for the sanctuary with funds from Emma Schlichting family organ fund.
1980 to 1982	All-church retreats held at Messiah College, Grantham, Pennsylvania.
May 17, 1982	Beryl Jantzi began service as Youth Pastor and served us for 4 years until 1986
1982	Formation of first Pastoral Team--Norma Johnson and Urbane Peachey, lay persons.
Summer 1982	AMC presentation of *Godspell*
1982	AMC Pictorial Directory was produced.
1984	Sponsorship of the Sanchez family
Sept. 15-16, 1984	25th year Anniversary celebration; membership was 339. Publication of anniversary booklet, *Akron Mennonite Church 1959-1984*

DATE	ACTIVITY
1985	Diamond Street Nursery School expanded to include day care in the newly constructed expansion of the education wing to become Diamond Street Preschool Center.
1985	Twenty-six AMC members plus children and other attending adults left AMC, as planned, to establish Community Mennonite Church of Lancaster.
1986	Production of *Cotton Patch Gospel.*
Sept. 7, 1986	Urbane Peachey became our Pastor. He had been an active member of AMC since 1965. He served us for 14 years until May 2000.
1986	Committee work began the restructuring of AMC following the congregation-wide study undertaken in 1985.
May 24, 1987	Groundbreaking for the new expansion of AMC.
Dec. 1988	Production of *Amahl and the Night Visitors.*
1987-1989	Fred Swartzentruber served as Youth Pastor for 2 years.
1989-1991	Paul Longacre served as Interim Associate Pastor for 2 years.
April 2, 1989	Dedication of new facility and celebration of 30th Anniversary of AMC; membership was 350.
1989	Formation of Arts and Symbols committee
Spring 1990	Performance of *The Holy City.*

DATE	ACTIVITY
1990	AMC Pictorial Directory was produced.
1990	Formation of Children's Ministry Team and Youth Ministry Team—Jr. MYF & MYF.
1991	First part-time Music Minister approved, Marcella Hostetler served 1 year.
1991	Six-week pastoral service of Sjbout Van der Meer from the Netherlands.
1991	Easter performance of Vivaldi's *Gloria*.
1991	Beginning of Men's Choir, singing once each month.
1991	MYF service project in Jamaica.
1991	Beryl Jantzi came to us as Associate Pastor and served 5 years until 1996.
1992	Roger Farmer invited to serve as a summer Pastoral Intern.
1992	Larry Penner served 2 years as Music Minister.
1992-93	Completed a double Habitat for Humanity house in Ephrata for two families.
1992	Head Start withdrew its daycare, giving DSPC expanded facilities to become DSECC.
1993	AMC Pictorial Directory was produced.
February 1994	Jan Miller served as Parish Nurse as a volunteer until 1997.
1994	Land Use – Shared Housing project (for senior housing on AMC campus) was not approved.

DATE	ACTIVITY
1994	Cheryl Eshleman served 4 years as Music Minister.
July 1996	Vacation Bible School – Marketplace 29 A.D.
	Administrator position approved; Melissa Roth served 6 years until 2000.
	Nancy Heisey serves in interim Preaching, Worship, and MYF Education position.
	Jeanette Bontrager serves as Pastoral Visitor.
1997	Sponsorship of the Gligorevic family. They have become AMC members.
Spring 1997	First Discernment Sunday--a process to replace congregational meetings.
September 1997	Dawn Yoder Harms came to us as Associate Pastor and is currently serving as Co-pastor.
1997-1998	AMC Pictorial Directory was produced.
1998	WMSC integrates with a program of Mennonite General Conference to become Mennonite Women
1998	Mary Ann Johnson served 4 years as Music Minister.
1999	Half-time Children's Christian Education Minister approved--Mary Jane Crockett was hired.
Sept. 19, 1999	Dawn Yoder Harms was ordained as Minister of the Gospel.

DATE	ACTIVITY
Oct. 2-3, 1999	Celebration of AMC's 40th Anniversary. It is of interest to note that 26 of the 46 charter members are active AMC members after 40 years.
May 31, 2000	Urbane Peachey retired as Pastor, having served 14 years.
July 2000	Jim S. Amstutz hired as Lead Pastor, with service to begin August 2001.
June 2000-Aug. 2001	Pastor Dawn Yoder Harms was supported by pastoral interim team: Lowell Detweiler, Gudrun Mathies, and Linda Helmus.
August 2000	Janet Weber begins position as Administrator.
August 1, 2001	Jim S. Amstutz begins term as Lead Pastor and is presently serving as Co-pastor.
July 2001	MYF attended the Nashville, Tennessee, Youth Convention.
	AMC hosted Atlantic Coast Conference Assembly.
	Remodeled kitchen.
January 2002	Vision Retreat I: Begin developing 5-year goals.
May 2002	DSECC incorporated.
June–August 2002	Sabbatical for Dawn Yoder Harms. Gudrun Mathies and Patrice Flaming serve as interim staff.
June 8, 2002	Mortgage burning for the third building program of AMC.
	Building committees: 1986-87: Rollin Rheinheimer, chair; 1987-89: Gerald Horst, chair; Glenn Weaver, chair of finance.

DATE	ACTIVITY
2003	*Vision*--Implementation of a 5 to10 year Master Plan for Vision and Growth of AMC.
January 2003	Patricia Martin hired as Music Minister.
September 2003	*Vision*—Discipleship Hour replaces Christian Education Hour.
	Vision—Changed order of service: Discipleship Hour at 9:00 a.m. for one year.
	Vision—Ministry Teams begun as part of new organizational structure.
Easter 2003	Choir: Brahms: *A German Requiem.*
Summer 2003	MYF attended Mennonite Youth Convention in Atlanta, Georgia.
November 2003	*Vision*—Hired architectural consultant to study facilities and land use.
January 2004	Ministry Team sponsored Rybaltouski family from Russia.
July 2004	Vacation Bible School *Marketplace 29 A.D.* for children.
November 2004	Men's Choir program honored Warren Leatherman for 14 years of musical leadership.
December 2004	AMC members participated in MDS hurricane recovery project in Century, Florida.
2005	AMC Pictorial Directory produced.
Summer 2005	MYF participated in hurricane recovery project with MDS in Arcadia, Florida.

DATE	ACTIVITY
Summer 2005	Jim S. Amstutz sabbatical: Richard Weaver and Betsy Headrick McCrae assisted with pastoral duties.
February 2006	Vision Retreat II
April 2006	*Vision*—A vote to move forward with building project to build a new kitchen and activity center and remodel the fellowship hall for Christian Education space did not receive needed two-thirds vote and project was tabled.
Summer 2006	MYF SWAP project in Harlan, Kentucky.
Summer 2007	Dawn Yoder Harms on sabbatical: Betsy Headrick McCrae on staff during Dawn's absence. MYF attended Mennonite Youth Convention in San Jose, California.
Sept. 2007	Special Care Minister, Jeanette Bontrager, hired—10 hours a week—and served until December 2008.
November 2007	AMC 50-Year Anniversary Committee begins meeting: Bob Wyble (chair), Ed Miller, Gerald Kaufman, Renny Magill, and Janet Weber, committee members.
January 2008	Vision Retreat III
February 2008	Dawn Yoder Harms went to Argentina as AMC pastoral representative with Argentina Partnership.
May 2008	MYF cookbook was produced and sold to raise funds for work projects.

DATE	ACTIVITY
July 2008	MYF traveled to New Orleans, Louisiana, for work project.
July 2008	Child Protection Policy activated.
September 2008	Ministry team sponsored the Jabri family from Iraq.
Nov 5-Dec 13, 2008	AMC participated in MDS' Partnership Home Program in Cameron, Louisiana.
March 10, 2009	Pastor Dawn Yoder Harms announced her resignation, effective December 31, 2009.
May 2009	AMC Pictorial Directory produced.
Summer 2009	Summer Bible School—*Marketplace 29 A.D.* for children.
	Jim S. Amstutz on sabbatical. Sara Wiegner will add pastoral support.
Sept 26-27, 2009	Celebration of AMC's 50th Anniversary. As of this date, 24 of the 46 charter members are active AMC members.

COMMITMENT AND COVENANT STATEMENTS

AKRON MENNONITE CHURCH
MEMBERSHIP COMMITMENT
April 1960

The basis of membership is an experience with Christ as Savior and a commitment to Him as Lord and Master, which is expressed by loyalty and service in fellowship with a local body of believers.

To effectively promote the Christian life in ourselves and to those around us,we thus commit ourselves to the following:

1. RESPONSIBILITY TO THE FELLOWHIP
    We believed the Christian is called to a committed fellowship of believers. Thus we pledge ourselves to the other members of this group to share openly our problems and concerns, to care for the spiritual and physical needs of each other and to make this fellowship a vital part of our life. Working out the problems of church life, Christian ethics, and church discipline will be the task of the entire group. Members are expected to be present at group meetings that will be held frequently by decision of the group. Group decisions will be binding on the members.

2. WORSHIP
    We believe the Christian is called to regular public and private worship of God. Thus we pledge ourselves to attendance at all worship and other scheduled meetings of the congregation. We also pledge ourselves to the regular family and private worship.

3. CHRISTIAN NURTURE
    We believe the Christian is called to a basic knowledge of the Holy Scriptures. Thus we pledge ourselves to continued study of the Bible and good Christian literature. We also pledge ourselves

to a vital Christian education program to include Sunday School, Summer Bible School, regular Bible study group experiences, and study conferences on a graded level.

4. MATERIAL GOODS

We believe all our material things belong to God and we are ready to have the fellowship guide us in the best stewardship of these possessions. As part of our stewardship, we will pledge to give liberally of our total income for the work of the Christian church.

5. WITNESS AND SERVICE

We believe that we are responsible to actively seek to win men to salvation and to demonstrate our concern for man's total needs. Thus we pledge to allow sufficient time for work of the congregation to involve ourselves, on a scheduled basis, in the outreach of the congregation, realizing that this may conflict with an already busy schedule. We also dedicate ourselves to the promotion of the concept of voluntary service by influence through the home and church.

6. RESPONSIBILITY TO CONFERENCE

We believe we are responsible to the larger conference body to give and to receive counsel and direction for effectively promoting our congregational life and practice. Thus we pledge ourselves to support the practice and program of the Ohio and Eastern Mennonite Conference,

AKRON MENNONITE CHURCH
DISCIPLINES OF MEMBERSHIP
March 1968

Membership in the Akron Mennonite Church means involvement in the fellowship of God's people which lives to celebrate the past, present and future relevance of Jesus Christ and assumes the weighty responsibility of bringing wholeness to the total man in our broken world. We understand this to mean all those ways by which Christians witness to the reality of God in Jesus Christ and thereby make know His power and love to the world.

As members of this congregation, we covenant individually and collectively to live by the following disciplines.

CONGREGATONAL LIFE: Members participate regularly in the worship and mission of the congregation. Members assist and uphold each other in times of need, agree to give and receive counsel, fellowship with others and respect each other regardless of differences. The congregation discusses openly matters affecting its life and members agree to work in harmony with official actions of the congregation. Working out the strategy for congregational life, witness and church discipline is the congregation's constant task.

MINISTRY: Members are the ministers of the church. Members liberally use their spiritual gifts and make known in their vocations and every relationship the source and meaning of their Christian life. Because members believe God is at work in their communities, they seek to live Christ-like there and participate in tasks of community betterment.

RECONCILIATION: Members experience the reconciling work of God in Jesus Christ, and therefore seek to bring reconciliation to those who are separated by social, economic, racial and national barriers. Members identify with the victims of such conflicts and actively pursue an equitable solution through peaceful means. Members witness to the brotherhood of all men under the Lordship of Christ.

STEWARDSHIP: Members are selective in their responses to claims made upon their time, energy and money so that generous and increasing resources may be volunteered for the deeper concerns.

NURTURE: Members grow in relationship with God and in awareness of His presence in their lives through Bible study, prayer and meditation. Members participate creatively in the educational opportunities of the church for spiritual and intellectual growth.

CHURCH UNIVERSAL: Members believe that they do not fully experience the "body of Christ" in the congregation alone. For this reason this congregation and its members seek to relate in meaningful ways to the Mennonite brotherhood, the churches of Lancaster County, and the world-wide Christian community.

As members of this congregation we seek the help of God and each other to achieve this covenant and God's purpose for us individually and collectively. We confess our failure to fully achieve this covenant and God's purpose for us. May the God whom we know through His revelation in Christ and the church be praised by our lives.

AKRON MENNONITE CHURCH
COVENANT OF MEMBERSHIP
October 1975

The basis of membership in the Akron Mennonite Church is a commitment to Jesus Christ as Savior and Lord. This is expressed with a local body of believers in service and witness to each other and to His world.

As members of this congregation we covenant to live by the following disciplines:

CONGREGATIONAL LIFE: We believe our congregation is a part of the body of Christ and therefore should be the principal concern for each of us. This means responsible participation in worship service, Sunday school and congregational meetings. We expect that each member be accountable to a small group, or to at least one other member to openly share burdens, joys, growth and disciplines.

MINISTRY: We believe all members are ministers of the church. This means working inside of the congregation and outside of it. A defined task for each member is arrived at in counsel with the small group. We believe we should share the "Good News" and invite other into the Kingdom.

RECONCILIATION: We believe we have a duty of love to all peoples and want to identify with the victims of spiritual, social, economic, racial, and national conflicts. We will follow God's call to be peacemakers within the congregation, the community, and the world.

STEWARDSHIP: We recognize and want to resist the temptations of our affluent society. Realizing that both "tithing" and "as the Lord has prospered" are Biblical concepts, we believe we owe our Lord at least "one tenth" of our time, energy and earnings.

NURTURE: We will seek to grow in our Christian life by regular and careful Bible study, worship and prayer with our families and in private.

CHURCH UNIVERSAL: We believe that the "Body of Christ" is found wherever people recognize that Christ is Lord. We therefore wish to relate to and learn from other congregations of our denomination, the churches of our area and the worldwide Christian community.

RENEWAL: With the counsel of the small group, we will yearly examine our faithfulness and renew our covenant.

May God guide and bless us as we keep these promises and may He forgive and give us renewing grace when we fail.

AKRON MENNONITE CHURCH
January 1981

MISSION STATEMENT

We, the Akron Mennonite church, are a community of believers responding to God's love. We accept the Scriptures as our guide for faith and life. We believe in God the Creator, in Jesus Christ the Lord and Savior, and in the Holy Spirit, God's presence among us. We commit ourselves to being a model of Christ-likeness in a broken world. All our ministries are offered to the congregation and others as invitation to faith and service.

MEMBERSHIP COVENANT

The Christian covenant is a commitment to God and involves participation in the community of God's people. The basis of membership in the Akron Mennonite Church is a commitment to Jesus Christ as Savior and Lord. This is expressed with a local body of believers in service and witness to each other and to His world.

EXPECTATIONS:

CONGREGATIONAL LIFE: We believe our congregation is a part of the body of Christ and therefore should be the principal commitment for each of us. This means responsible participation in worship Service, Sunday School and congregational meetings. We expect that each member be accountable to a small group or to at least one other member to openly share burdens, joys, growth and disciplines.

MINISTRY: We believe all members are ministers of the church. This means working inside of the congregation and outside of it. Tasks of ministry for each member are arrived at in counsel with the small group. We believe we should share the "Good News" and invite other into the Kingdom.

RECONCILIATION: We believe we have a duty of love to all peoples and want to identify with the victims of spiritual, social, economic, racial, and national conflicts. We will follow God's call to be peacemakers within the congregation, the community, and the world. We expect each member to follow Christ's example of nonresistant love.

STEWARDSHIP: We recognize that all we are and have is a gift from God and we want to resist the temptations of our affluent society. Realizing that both "tithing" and "as the Lord has prospered" are Biblical concepts, we believe we owe our Lord at least one- tenth of our time, energy and earnings.

NURTURE: We will seek to grow in our Christian life by regular and careful Bible study, worship and prayer with our families and in private.

CHURCH UNIVERSAL: We believe that the "body of Christ" is found wherever people recognize that Jesus Christ is Lord. We therefore wish to relate to and learn from other congregations of our denomination, the churches of our area and the worldwide Christian community.

RENEWAL: With the counsel of other members of the congregation, we will examine yearly our faithfulness to the membership expectations and renew our covenant.

AKRON MENNONITE CHURCH
June 1996 to present

MISSION STATEMENT

We, the Akron Mennonite Church, are a community of believers responding to God's love. We accept the Scriptures as our guide for faith and life. We believe in God the Creator, in Jesus Christ the Lord and Savior, and in the Holy Spirit, God's presence among us. We commit ourselves to being a model of Christ-likeness in a broken world. All our ministries are offered to the congregation and others as invitation to faith and service.

CHURCH COVENANT

The Christian covenant is a commitment to God and the community of faith. The basis of membership in the Akron Mennonite Church is a commitment to Jesus Christ as Savior and Lord and a readiness to be a part of a body that strives to be a model of Christ-likeness in a broken world. We join in the covenant and commit ourselves to be in conversation about its meaning. All in our church community are encouraged to join in this covenant even though the expectations are addressed to members.

EXPECTATIONS:

CONGREGATIONAL LIFE: We believe our congregation is a part of the body of Christ and therefore should be a priority for each of us. This means regular participation in the worship Service, Sunday school and congregational meetings, and selected ministries where one is nurtured and where one's gift's can be used in kingdom work. We expect each person to be in a sharing relationship with a small group or with at least one other person in the congregation.

MINISTRY: We believe all members are ministers of the church. Tasks of ministry for each person grow out of gift discernment in the congregation. We are committed to sharing the Good News and inviting other into the Kingdom.

RECONCILIATION: We believe we are called to love all peoples and want to identify with the victims of spiritual, social, economic, racial, and national conflicts. We will follow God's call to be peacemakers within the congregation, the community, and the world. We expect each person to follow Christ's example of nonresistant love.

STEWARDSHIP: We recognize that all we are and have is a gift from God and we want to resist the materialistic temptations of our affluent society. Realizing that both tithing and *as the Lord has prospered* are biblical concepts, we believe we owe our Lord at least one-tenth of our time, energy and earnings.

NURTURE: We will seek to grow in our Christian life through the practice of spiritual disciplines such as Bible study, worship and nurture in Christian education, relationships and prayer.

CHURCH UNIVERSAL: We believe that the body of Christ is found wherever people recognize that Jesus Christ is Lord. We therefore wish to relate to and learn from other congregations of our denomination, the churches of our area and the worldwide Christian community.

RENEWAL: We will, with the counsel of others in the church, annually examine our practice of these expectations and renew our commitment to them.

AKRON MENNONITE CHURCH
2002

VISION STATEMENT

VISION FOR AMC: Akron Mennonite Church will be fully engaged in God's mission in a broken world as we are called, equipped and sent by the Holy Spirit to follow Christ in life. Shaped by the gifts and vision of our members, we will keep Christ and church at the center of our lives as we reach out to neighbors near and far and witness to the world around us through an Anabaptist-Mennonite expression of faith.

Bibliography

Akron Mennonite Church Archives
   Annual reports, minutes, correspondence and directories

Akron Mennonite Church 25th anniversary booklet, 1984.

Akron Mennonite Church 40th anniversary booklet, 1999.

Akron Mennonite Church Collection (III-38-125), Mennonite Church USA Archives, Goshen, IN.

Boers, Paul, *The Way is Made for Walking: A Pilgrimage Along the Camino de Santiago*, Intervarsity Press, Downers Grove, IL 2007.

Borough of Akron, 75th Anniversary, 1895-1970, Akron, PA.

Brenneman, Robert, "Embodied Forgiveness: Yoder and the (Body) Politics of Footwashing" Mennonite Quarterly Review, (January, 2009) Goshen, IN.

Bruce, F.F, *New International Bible Commentary*, Pickering & Inglis, Zondervan, Grand Rapids, MI, 1979.

Detweiler, Lowell, *The Hammer Rings Hope,* Herald Press, Scottdale, PA, 2000.

Forest Hills Mennonite Church 40TH Anniversary 1946-1986, Leola, PA.

Hymnal, A Worship Book, Mennonite Publishing House, Scottdale, PA. 1992

Kanagy, Conrad L., *Road Signs for the Journey, A Profile of Mennonite Church USA,* Herald Press, Scottdale, PA 2007.

Kraybill, Nelson, J., *On the Pilgrims' Way,* Herald Press, Scottdale, PA, 1990.

Leatherman, Paul, *A Full and Rewarding Life: A Memoir,* Self-Published, Akron, PA, 2004.

Longacre, Doris Janzen, *Living more with less,* Herald Press, Scottdale, PA, 1980.

Longacre, Doris Janzen, *More-with-Less Cookbook,* Herald Press, Scottdale, PA, 1976.

Meeks, Wayne A, *The First Urban Christians,* Yale University Press, New Haven, CT, 1983.

O.N. Johns Collection (Hist.Mss. 1-234, Box 2), Mennonite Church USA Archives, Goshen, IN.

Peterson, Eugene H., *The Message, The Bible in Contemporary Language,* Navepress, Colorado Springs, CO, 2002.

Ruth, John, *The Earth is the Lord's,* Herald Press, Scottsdale, PA, 2001.

The Holy Bible, New Revised Standard Version, World Publishing, Grand Rapids, MI, 1989.

White, L. Michael, *Building God's House in the Roman World, Architectural Adoption among Pagans, Jews and Christians,* Johns Hopkins University Press, Baltimore, MD, 1990.

Wright, Robert, "One World Under God," *The Atlantic Monthly,* (April 2009).

Interviews

Diener, Menno, Akron, Pennsylvania

Ebersole, Ginny, Lititz, Pennsylvania

Gingerich, Gladys, Lititz, Pennsylvania

Johns, David, Son of O.N. Johns, Goshen, Indiana

Hershberger, June, Director of Diamond Street Early Childhood Center, Akron Pennsylvania

Hess, David and Ruth, Ephrata, Pennsylvania

Horst, Carolyn, Akron, Pennsylvania

Hostetler, John and Kathy, Ephrata, Pennsylvania

Kuniholm, Jason, Minister of Congregational Life, Mellingers Mennonite Church, Lancaster, Pennsylvania

Ruth, John, Historian, Harleysville, Pennsylvania

Snader, Nevin, Akron, Pennsylvania

Thomas, Robert, Tabor Community Services, Lancaster, Pennsylvania

Weaver, Anne and Glenn, New Holland, Pennsylvania

Wenger, A Grace, Founder of Menno Housing, Retired Teacher, Lititz, Pennsylvania

Zehr, Paul, Theologian, Lancaster, Pennsylvania

Gerald Kaufman, 2008.

About the Author

Gerald W. Kaufman was born in Johnstown, PA. He graduated from Goshen College, Goshen, Indiana, in 1961 and received a MSW from Indiana University, Indianapolis, Indiana, 1965. He and his wife Marlene have been members of Akron Mennonite Church since 1969. They are retired social workers and counselors. They have four children and eleven grandchildren.

Gerald and Marlene are the authors of *Freedom Fences, How to set limits that free you to enjoy your marriage and family,* published in 1999. Their daughters, Anne Kaufman Weaver and Nina Kaufman Harnish, were co-authors. In 2005, Gerald and Marlene authored *Monday Marriage, Celebrating the Ordinary.* Herald Press, Scottdale, Pennsylvania, published both books.

Index